C000156364

HOW TO SEI
DEMYST...IED

PRCA PROFESSIONAL

Series Editor

Nick Wallwork, Emerald Publishing

The Public Relations and Communications Association (PRCA) is the world's largest professional PR body, representing more than 35,000 PR professionals in 82 countries worldwide. If you wish to improve your knowledge and understanding of PR practice and theory, this series from *Emerald Publishing*, created in conjunction with the most accomplished PRCA experts, is for you.

Previously Published

The Art of Leadership through Public Relations by Patrik Schober

HOW TO SELL VALUE – DEMYSTIFIED

A Practical Guide for Communications Agencies

BY

CRISPIN MANNERS
Onva Consulting, UK

United Kingdom – North America – Japan – India
Malaysia – China

Emerald Publishing Limited
Emerald Publishing, Floor 5, Northspring, 21-23 Wellington Street, Leeds LS1 4DL

First edition 2023

Reprints and permissions service
Contact: www.copyright.com

British Library Cataloguing in Publication Data
A catalogue record for this book is available from the British Library

ISBN: 978-1-83797-125-1 (Print)
ISBN: 978-1-83797-122-0 (Online)
ISBN: 978-1-83797-124-4 (Epub)

Printed and bound by CPI Group (UK) Ltd, Croydon, CR0 4YY

INVESTOR IN PEOPLE

This book is dedicated to my beautiful granddaughter, Emily.

CONTENTS

LIST OF FIGURES

LIST OF ABBREVIATIONS AND ACRONYMS

Introduction – PRCA   Public Relations and Communications Association

SCARF   A brain-based model for collaborating with and influencing others. The individual letters stand for:

S – Status
C – Certainty
A – Autonomy
R – Relatedness
F – Fairness

SEO   Search Engine Optimisation

ACKNOWLEDGEMENTS

I would like to thank my wife Juliet for her daily support and encouragement, and my two sons, Matt and Philip for the inspiration they provide in the way they rise to life's challenges and opportunities. My colleague Marta needs a special mention, not just for her help with this book but also for making the work we do together so enjoyable.

I'm also very grateful to the PRCA, and the team at Emerald, for their support in making this book possible.

I'd like to thank the Partners of the Worldcom PR Group and in particular Todd Lynch for the willingness to embrace new ways of working.

Finally, I would like to thank all the owners of the agencies I have helped. By sharing your challenges with me, and being willing to explore new ways to achieve success, you have inspired me to capture what we have learnt together in this book. Special mention needs to go to my long-time friends and agency owners, Diego Biasi and Patrik Schober. I also would like to mention Leigh Greenwood, Henry Griffiths, Jonathan Andrews, Julie Moulsdale, Lesley Singleton and Martina Quinn for the way they have embraced the purpose-driven approach I believe is so pivotal to business success.

I hope it helps great agencies to earn the rewards they deserve by becoming more outcome and value focused.

INTRODUCTION – THE BUSINESS CASE FOR SELLING VALUE, NOT TIME

I've written this book because I see wonderful PR people delivering miracles for their clients every day – and not getting the rewards they deserve.

The reason for this is simple. Over the last few decades, PR people have trained themselves, and their clients, to focus on activity over outcomes, and on time rather than value. In fact, while writing this book, the Public Relations and Communications Association (PRCA)[1] published research which shows that 83% of agencies do not sell by value.

Why does that matter? It matters because the PR sector is known for long hours, stressful work, insufficient time and money to invest in personal development and the treadmill of winning clients only to overservice them.

So this book is designed to help people chart a way out of this painful cycle, by adopting a change in behaviour that makes the work they do more intellectually, emotionally and financially rewarding.

While some chapters of the book may, at first, appear to be targeted at senior levels in an agency, my goal is to show everyone in an agency how they can get a greater sense of achievement and fulfilment by moving to a value-based model.

WHY CHANGE NOW?

The need to change behaviour now is more urgent because of the impact of three significant challenges:

- The global pandemic encouraged people of all ages to question why they do things, and to seek purpose in what they do. Without a focus on delivering value, it is very hard to feel that what you do is worth the effort, which is discouraging some people from pursuing or continuing a career in PR.

- The aftermath of the pandemic, exacerbated by the impact of the war in Ukraine, has created a period of high inflation and low growth – what was dubbed 'stagflation' in the 1970s. In a period of such economic uncertainty, organisations change the way they buy. The leaders of those organisations become much more focused on the value they will receive than they are in a buoyant market. In other words, they are only prepared to invest in things that will deliver a clear and **certain** return on investment.

Agency owners, and in-house teams, often misread this as a desire by an organisation's leadership to reduce costs. But the reason clients decide to reduce budgets, or dispense with agency, or in-house PR services completely, is because they cannot see, with **certainty**, what value they get from their investment.

At the heart of this change in leadership behaviour is one question: '*Why does that matter?*' It's a question that will feature throughout this book, as it is a question that PR people, at all levels, should make the foundation for their journey towards being value-driven. It's a question that seeks proof of business/organisational value, something that demonstrably helps an organisation to achieve its priority objectives or outcomes.

But the 'proof' provided by most PR people today is activity based rather than outcome based. An answer by an in-house PR manager that says, '*we got some brilliant press coverage*', just won't cut it with leadership. It will be met by the same question. *Why does that matter?* And without compelling proof of a return on investment, leaders will simply decide not to risk wasting their money.

If PR people don't start proving the business value of what they do, the consequences (based on previous recessions) are likely to be loss of income and talent, and a significant impact on the future potential of the agency.

- Challenging times also drive innovation. In recent months, the Worldcom Confidence Index[2] https://worldcomgroup.com/confidence-index/has shown that business leaders are planning to invest in technology – particularly Artificial Intelligence (AI) – to solve the current economic challenges with disruptive solutions. One of the clients of an agency I advise recently sent through a draft release created by ChatGPT (an AI tool). It was a perfectly adequate release, and the covering email from the client said: '*It took just 15 seconds*'. If PR people define their value by WHAT they do – write a press release – rather than WHY they do it – achieve a business outcome – then they will have little defence against clients replacing them with tools like ChatGPT. Of course, agencies could use this technology to streamline more routine tasks, so they can focus on providing expert advice instead. After all, experts are valued more than practitioners.

The three challenges above create the need for PR people to adopt a disruptive approach to proving their value.

This book demystifies how to become more value-driven and to charge according to the value delivered. It offers PR people a choice of whether to adopt a new approach or to stick to what they know. If you choose to change your behaviour, then I hope you find this book a helpful guide for you and your colleagues on that journey. I believe it will make your agency, or in-house department, more resilient, flexible and successful.

THE NEED FOR A FUNDAMENTAL CHANGE IN BEHAVIOUR

Many of the people I talk to about selling value are looking for me to give them a simple-to-follow pricing algorithm that treats pricing value in the same way as pricing time. Pricing time is easy. You know how many people you have. You know how many hours they have to deliver work. You know your other costs. And you know how much profit you'd like to make. Then all you need to do is estimate how long something will take to deliver, and by whom, and you have a price.

But the cosy certainty this simple maths produces is fundamentally flawed for several reasons, including:

- The estimate of how much time something will take is often inaccurate (and frequently adjusted to create a price that will fit a client's budget).

- The work undertaken often doesn't reflect the proposal on which the price was based.

- Clients often ask for 'extra' activity that is delivered free of charge. The average overservicing rate for the sector is often quoted as being 20%. If that's correct, it means that one day in every individual's working week is given away free!

- The processes behind the way the work is delivered – such as the approach to calls and meetings – are inefficient. And often the time associated with these activities is not included in the pricing estimate.

But the biggest flaw in time-based pricing is its relationship to the value delivered.

If a 15-minute call opens an opportunity that converts to $1 million of value for a client, does it make sense to charge for 15 minutes? Conversely, if it takes eight hours to write a dull press release, that won't get picked up, is it worth eight hours of fee?

BEING SCARED OF COMMITTING TO RESULTS

So what is behind the unwillingness to price according to value? The answer is complex, but includes the following oft quoted phrases:

- *'We cannot guarantee results.'*

- *'We aren't the only contributor to an outcome.'*

If you are a leader who is seeking certainty of value, it's easy to see why these phrases won't persuade you to spend money. You will most likely compare the intangible effect PR agencies promise with the tangible effect of other marketing disciplines, such as pay per click advertising.

In reality, the word **guarantee** means being able to show a cause and effect in advance. Pay per click guarantees a click through and makes clear its role in a process. What it doesn't guarantee is the quality of the click or what happens after the click through. But in the absence of PR guaranteeing anything, or demonstrating what role it has in the journey to an important outcome, it's easy to see why budgets may be diverted towards something that appears more *certain.*

So charging for the value you deliver must start with the business or organisational outcome your work helps to deliver. And many clients make that hard to do, because the creators of a budget do not write the PR brief for the people within their own organisation who spend it.

WHY NOT JUST WEATHER THE STORM?

There have been plenty of recessions over the last 50 years and yet the PR market has grown. So why is a change in behaviour needed now? Why can't we just weather the current storm and carry on as normal?

The answer is, of course, that you can. But is that the best strategy?

In 2010, the *Harvard Business Review* published an article entitled 'Roaring out of Recession'.[3] The article reviewed how organisations responded to previous recessions and the impact this had on their performance after the recession was over.

This extract demonstrates why it is so important to make the right choice now. *'Seventeen percent of the companies in our study didn't survive a recession. The survivors were painfully slow to recover from the battering. About 80% of them had not yet regained their pre-recession growth rates for sales and profits three years after a recession. Only a small number of companies – approximately 9% of our sample – flourished after a slowdown, doing better on key financial parameters than they had before it and outperforming rivals in their industry by at least 10% in terms of sales and profits growth.'*

The researchers who wrote the article identified four basic behaviours: prevention, promotion, pragmatic and progressive. The *prevention* focused companies tried to cut their way out of trouble by reducing expenditure and investment. These companies performed the worst after the recession, with only half the sales growth, and a third of the profit growth, of *progressive* companies.

So what defines the approach of the *progressive* organisations?

They combine a focus on operational efficiency, i.e. eliminating waste from the way things are done, rather than cutting people, with investment in new ways to satisfy customer needs. Their post-recession growth in sales and earnings is the best among the groups in the study. In short, they changed the way the business operated to be more compelling to their customers. They were the ones that came *'roaring out of recession'*.

So that is the opportunity facing you. The chance to take a progressive approach to secure your future, by eliminating waste from the way you operate, and presenting and pricing your services according to how they deliver greater certainty of value to clients.

If you want to transform the performance of your agency by becoming more outcome and value focused, then read on.

1

THE EIGHT DEADLY SINS OF TIME-BASED PRICING

To call the actions below a sin is obviously over the top. Nobody is going to punish you for choosing to continue to 'sell time'.

What this chapter aims to do is to challenge the accepted wisdom that 'selling time' is the most effective way to achieve success for your agency. It's not.

Obviously, there are thousands of agencies around the world that are successful and use the time-based model. But they could be even more successful if they adopted a value-based approach.

The problem with 'selling time' is that it leaves significant value 'on the table', value that your agency will have created for the client, and for which you should be rewarded.

There are lots of flaws in a time-based approach. Some are explored below.

SIN #1 – THINKING THAT TIME IS, BY DEFINITION, VALUABLE

The interesting thing about the time-based model is that it implies that time is, in and of itself, valuable. This is not the case. What is valuable is how an individual uses that time to achieve something of value.

What is perhaps more important is whether clients demonstrate that they value time more than the value of what the time produces. In most cases they do not.

Imagine your agency estimated that it will take 30 hours to attract 15 journalists to a launch press event. But it took your team 60 hours to do so because they found it much harder to secure attendance by the required number of journalists. How many clients will pay you for the extra 30 hours? Probably none. Their attitude will be that how long it takes to deliver the 15 journalists is your problem. Imagine if your team were super successful and secured the required attendance in just 10 hours. Will your client care and audit the time taken? No – because as far as they are concerned, you delivered what you promised.

Once you recognise that time has no intrinsic value, but the outcome from the time spent does, you are already on the path to pricing according to the value you deliver, rather than the time you expend.

SIN #2 – FAILING TO LINK WHAT YOU DO TO AN OUTCOME THE CLIENT VALUES

I recently saw a statement of work (SOW) produced by a very good agency as part of a proposal. The SOW had a long list of actions but no mention of the outcome the client wanted to achieve. It had hours allocated per month to different people in the team – effectively a bucket of time to be used to deliver the actions. This then translated to a pricing page which was called a budget. The budget identified a number of outputs from the budget, e.g. number of cuttings and guidance on messaging.

Nowhere was the 'budget' connected to the client's reason to invest – to break into a new market and succeed on arrival. And nowhere were the various campaigns that were part of the proposal referred to in the SOW. So the prospective client would be left to assume that they were buying time and cuttings. What if the prospect looked at the SOW and asked: *'Why do those cuttings matter?'* There was no explicit answer in the SOW.

The weakness of this approach was further compounded by the agency adopting a gold, silver, bronze approach to the pricing. This is used by lots of agencies to show how more time buys more services. Seems reasonable, until you ask why the extra time matters. If the prospect thinks the proposal is designed to help them succeed on arrival in a new market, then the bronze budget should achieve that outcome. What then would the silver and gold budgets achieve?

When you go into a car showroom, you aren't going to buy the time of someone to put your car together; you are going to buy the outcome of that process, a car. The dealer doesn't have a sign on the car saying 'Budget £35,000'. It's the price.

You don't ask the salesperson to list the costs of the components that make up the car and the time it takes to put the components together. You have one goal in mind to buy a car. If the salesperson said, I *can give you a year's supply of tyres* when you want a car, you'd think they were crazy. So why do we put a price on delivering a bunch of cuttings, when what the client wants to buy is 'success on arrival in a new market'? It's because we don't explicitly link what we do to an outcome the client values.

I know some of you will be thinking that we can't promise that we will deliver the outcome because there will be other contributors. That's true. But we can identify our vital, and pivotal, part in achieving that outcome – in this example, success on arrival in a new market.

Once you connect everything you do to the priority outcome a client wants to achieve, it's possible to price your contribution to achieving the outcome.

SIN #3 – THINKING YOU ARE SELLING TIME WHEN YOU GIVE MUCH OF IT AWAY FREE

In 2019, a *PRWeek* article, entitled: 'PR's overservicing epidemic: 90% of agencies overservice client accounts', said: '*The communications industry is in the grip of an "overservicing epidemic" as agencies desperate to please clients "promise the earth" and cannot say "no". The problem is causing nearly a fifth of staff to consider quitting*'.[1]

Three years later, a PRCA study, in May 2022, said of overservicing: '*Worries include fears relating to the troubling practice of over-servicing. This has been a consistent blight on the industry and is the subject of a new PRCA member consultation*'.[2]

The dictionary definition of overservicing is: '*to service someone unnecessarily or to an excessive degree*'. The words *unnecessarily* and *excessive* are interesting because they highlight how pointless overservicing is. But the definition should also include another important factor – the fact that the unnecessary and excessive service is **delivered free of charge!**

As the introduction says, the average overservicing rate for the sector is often quoted as being 20%. But at a recent workshop I ran for a large international agency, the range of overservicing disclosed ranged from -20% to $+270\%$!

Nearly all agencies give huge chunks of time away free. If they valued their time, then they would charge for every minute they expended.

So why do agencies price their services using time? Because, as the introduction suggests, it seems easier to do it that way than to price according to the value delivered. But pricing according to time sustains rather than eradicates the overservicing blight.

As the same *PR Week* article says, overservicing is often achieved by staff working unpaid overtime.

Put bluntly, bad pricing practice only delivers acceptable profit by taking advantage of employees. It's no wonder the study says 20% of people have considered quitting their agency.

If you want to eradicate overservicing from your business, calculate the total value of the time you give away free. Then calculate how much of that is delivered free by your people, i.e. unpaid overtime. Those two numbers should provide you with compelling financial and human reasons for the need to change.

Once you realise the lost business opportunity, and the human cost of continuing to price based on time, you will have compelling reasons to move to pricing by the value you deliver.

SIN #4 – BEING CONSTRAINED BY THE WORD 'RETAINER' WHICH ENCOURAGES THE WRONG ATTITUDE FROM CLIENTS AND AGENCIES

Agencies like 'retainers' because they give security of regular income. But apart from that benefit, retainers are generally unhelpful to an agency because they are a very ineffective way to define the value exchange between an agency and a client.

Retainers are simply a name for a contract. They usually define the monthly price and the duration. But the value that will be delivered is rarely explicitly defined. This leads clients to expect a consistent level of service every month because they are charged the same fee every month and see this fee as equating to a set number of days. In busy months, clients tend to ignore the extra effort. In quiet months they tend to ask for more to be done so they 'don't lose out on the days they've paid for'. Agencies tell me that this situation becomes progressively worse the longer they have a retained client.

So what's the reason for this behaviour? It's caused by Sin #2 – failing to link what you do to an important client outcome. And then, failing to set expectations about how the level of work to deliver that outcome changes across the year.

When I've discussed this with agencies, some say that it's hard to link what they do under a retainer with a client outcome. All this means is that the agency is NOT asking the magic question: Why does that matter? And because the agency doesn't ask it, the client doesn't either.

The net result is that the agency becomes seen as arms and legs the client doesn't want on the payroll, rather than experts they can't afford to have on the payroll.

The solution is to ask every client to define their top three business priorities in priority order. This enables you to define, in a SOW, what you will do to contribute to achieving those business priorities – and how this is spread across the year. This sets clear expectations with the client about *why* you are doing what you do and how this will create peaks and troughs of activity.

Because business priorities change, I recommend that you set expectations with each client that you will ask them to restate their business priorities once a quarter – so that you can adapt what you do to ensure it delivers the right business value – and update the SOW accordingly. It's obviously your choice about how frequently you ask for this information. But clients often change priorities without telling the agency – thus allowing you to continue work in areas they no longer value.

I also recommend that you change the name of your contract from a retainer to a service contract.

Once you have defined what you do in a way that is connected to a valued business outcome, it's possible to capture this in a service contract that sets client expectations more effectively.

SIN #5 – FAILING TO IDENTIFY WHAT IS NOT INCLUDED

An explicit SOW is only one part of the solution to being more in control of what is expected under a 'retainer' contract.

I recommend that you provide every client a companion document which explains what is NOT included in the SOW.

Most agencies think what isn't included is implicit in their SOW. If it's not listed, it's not included – right? But we know from the overservicing problem that clients don't see it this way. Because it's not clear what isn't included, and they think they are buying time not a specific outcome, they ask for extra, out of scope, work to be done.

By providing an explicit document that explains what is not included, you achieve two valuable things:

- You show clients all the other services that they are not currently accessing. This is very important, as I've lost count of the number of times agency owners have told me how annoyed they are that a current client just hired another agency to do something they have in their service mix.

- You set expectations that asking for any of these services will require additional money.

Once you have defined what is not included, it makes it easier for you to be more in control of overservicing, and it gives your team a platform for saying NO when a client asks for out-of-scope work to be carried out.

SIN #6 – ALLOCATING TEAM TIME FOR ACTIVITIES NOT OUTCOMES

If you quantify what you do in units of time rather than a valuable outcome, this leads to another bad practice, i.e. members of a client account team being allocated time to spend on tasks rather than on achieving outcomes. For example, it's quite common for a team member to be allocated a certain number of hours at the beginning of a week to use on tasks like writing a release or carrying out a media sell-in. Not surprisingly, the team member then spends the time as directed – often without achieving anything of real value.

A more effective approach would be to ask the individual to deliver certain outputs (as steps towards an outcome). So, instead of asking someone to do a sell-in to a long list of contacts, they could be asked to find a way to get coverage in a small number of high priority publications and stop once they've achieved that – the goal being to get the most value for the client from the least effort by the team.

This may seem like a semantic point, but the difference is quite profound in terms of how people use their time. The first request encourages people to see their job as using up time. The second request gets them to focus on working smarter to deliver a priority outcome. This will enhance their own sense of status, as its clear that they make a valuable contribution to the client and the agency.

Once you focus on outcomes, and the outputs which are steps on the journey to an outcome, everyone in the team starts to understand their responsibility in delivering value to a client. This encourages people to focus on delivering value with the least effort, because it is the value that matters, not how long it takes to deliver it.

SIN #7 – FAILING TO REMOVE SIGNIFICANT TIME DRAINS – SO YOU CAN FOCUS ON DELIVERING VALUE AND DEVELOPING YOUR PEOPLE

When I ask agency leaders about why they haven't developed the skills of their people, or focused on making processes more effective so they can deliver more value from less effort, one of the most common answers is the lack of time to do so.

And yet, every agency I know persists in allowing significant 'time drains' to continue unaddressed. When I ask junior PR consultants to identify processes that take up a lot of time, but deliver relatively little value in return, they immediately identify meetings and reporting.

Agency leaders often identify the same processes, but rarely have calculated the cost of the time wasted. And, because they haven't identified the time that can be freed up, they haven't worked out how that available time can be used to their advantage.

This failure to crystallise both the cost of time wasted, and the opportunity cost of not using time more productively, is one of the reasons why things don't change.

I have developed a very simple *'wasted time calculator'* to show how small changes to processes can free up huge quantities of time that can be used more productively. In Chart 1[3] below, you can see how this tool calculates the amount of time that can be saved by changing the frequency of calls with clients from weekly to fortnightly. In this example, I show how the time saved per person (from one to four people) increases with the number of clients.

Agencies seem to have the habit of setting the default duration of meetings at one hour, and also asking all members of the client team to be present on every call. So imagine you have an agency with 40 clients and client teams that have four people. If you shift every client from weekly to fortnightly calls, you will save 2.5 consultant years. Yes, you will save the time of two and a half people!

Imagine what you could do with 2.5 years of free time.

Imagine if you also changed the duration of the calls to 30 minutes rather than 60 minutes and allowed one team member to drop off a call, on a rotating basis. The cumulative impact in terms of time freed would be transformational in terms of productivity, profitability, personal development and team happiness.

Time saved by changing weekly calls to fortnightly					Saving in number of consultant years	
Call duration - 1 hour	**1 Person**	**2 People**	**3 People**	**4 People**		
Hours saved per annum per client by moving from weekly to fortnightly	**25**	**50**	**75**	**100**		
8 hour days saved per client	**3.125**	**6.25**	**9.375**	**12.5**		
Days saved for 4 clients	12.5	25	37.5	50		
Days saved for 6 clients	18.75	37.5	56.25	75		
Days saved for 8 clients	25	50	75	100		
Days saved for 10 clients	31.25	62.5	93.75	125	0.63	consultant years saved by moving to fortnightly if 4 people and 10 clients
Days saved for 20 clients	62.5	125	187.5	250	1.25	consultant years saved by moving to fortnightly if 4 people and 20 clients
Days saved for 40 clients	125	250	375	500	2.50	consultant years saved by moving to fortnightly if 4 people and 40 clients
Billable days for person year	**200**					
365 days less weekends, bank holidays, annual holiday half day per work week for training etc						

©Crispin Manners

Chart 1. Wasted Time Calculator – Time Saved by Changing Weekly Calls to Fortnightly.

CREATING AN EFFECTIVE MEETINGS PROTOCOL

Just releasing time isn't going to ensure that you achieve significant performance improvements. It will also be necessary to ensure that you have effective processes in place to make any changes sustainable. For example, if you cut the duration of meetings, it will be important to have an effective meetings protocol for everyone to follow. It will also make sense to make sure this approach to meetings brings to life your purpose (*why*) and proposition (*how*).

I recommend you break a meetings protocol into three stages – before, during and after the meeting, and define what needs to be done, by whom, at each stage. Chart 2[4] shows the 'before' phase of a sample protocol. A downloadable copy is available.[5]

Meetings Best Practice - Steps To Follow (Extract)

Steps to take	Names and detail	Actions taken
Before the meeting		
1. Always have a clear Purpose for the meeting i.e. explain at the outset/before the meeting why the meeting is being held and what is the outcome expected from the meeting		
2. Identify who should be invited and why - it is essential they are there / what their role in the meeting will be. Do not invite people for the sake of it as this hurts productivity and meeting effectiveness		
3. Make sure everyone who attends understands the Purpose and their role in the meeting		
4. Assign responsibilities for key parts of the meeting or steps towards achieving the meeting outcome		
a) Who will **lead the meeting** and what communication style do they need to adopt? For example, a brainstorm to collect ideas will need a very involving style that encourages people to share their ideas		
b) Who will ensure **everyone participates**		
c) Who will ensure the meeting **stays on track and achieves its outcome**		
d) Who will ensure that the meeting **finishes on time or early**		
e) Who will **record the decisions and the action responsibilities and deadlines**		

©Crispin Manners

Chart 2. Meetings Best Practice – Steps to Follow (Extract).

USING THE TIME FREED TO ADVANTAGE

So let's take just one of those changes – reducing the call duration from 60 to 30 minutes. Imagine if rather than just leaving the meeting after 30 minutes, you use the 30 minutes freed up to coach people on the team on how best to deliver the actions agreed in the meeting. This will instantly transform the personal development of your team, as it gives them frequent coaching on how to work smarter.

The benefits of this coaching are obvious. It demonstrates to the individual that you are investing in them. It enables leaders to delegate more effectively, confident that the team has the skills and confidence required to deliver what is expected. And it shows clients that they do not need to rely on the most senior person in the team, because the rest of the team are fully capable of doing what is required.

Imagine if you adopted the same approach to eliminate other time drains such as email habits, client reports and inefficient pitch processes, and converted the freed time to more productive uses. The ability to use the time available to deliver value to clients will be transformational.

Once you have identified your major time drains, you can work out the simplest ways to remove them, and how to use the time freed to everyone's advantage.

SIN #8 – FAILING TO STOP WORK ONCE AN OUTCOME HAS BEEN DELIVERED

One of the other problems that allocating team members a certain amount of time to expend is that they usually make sure that they do so. If their brief is to deliver priority outputs, or outcomes, in the shortest amount of time, they would stop once they achieved the required results.

When I suggest this approach to agency leaders, I am often met with objections that this is not ethical, because they are contracted to provide a certain amount of time. This answer highlights one of the many weaknesses of contracting to expend time, rather than to deliver outcomes of value.

If clients feel that it is unethical for an agency to stop work, once a result of value has been delivered, because there is time left to be utilised, they should similarly feel that it is unethical for them to ask for extra work to be delivered, if all the contracted time has been expended.

Contracting to deliver outcomes/outputs of value overcomes this dilemma, because time is no longer part of the equation. It also helps your team to seek guidance early if they feel that they are encountering problems that means the outcome may not be achieved.

Once you have identified and agreed the outcomes/outputs to be delivered, you can increase time effectiveness by enabling people to stop working once the outcomes have been delivered.

CHECKLIST

(1) Have you identified the outcome the client values most, that they are hiring you to help deliver?

(2) Have you developed a clear strategy for how you will deliver that outcome, and have you linked the price to the outcome and the strategy?

(3) Have you explicitly identified your part in delivering the desired outcome?

(4) Have you captured how you will deliver that outcome in an explicit SOW?

(5) Have you captured what is not included in a companion document to the SOW?

(6) Have you identified the value that the client expects to be delivered in terms of the outcomes they expect, and the outputs which are important steps on the journey to the outcome?

(7) Have you identified the client's top three business priorities?

(8) Have you allocated team tasks based on achieving the agreed outcomes, outputs and priorities – with the expectation that this is achieved in the least amount of time?

(9) Have you identified your major time drains, and calculated the cost to the business of not addressing them?

(10) Have you created effective replacement processes to the time drains you eliminate?

(11) Have you given a clear brief on the outcomes and outputs to be delivered and has been understood and accepted?

2

THE IMPORTANCE OF IDENTIFYING THE VALUE CLIENTS WANT

In the Introduction, I referred to research by the PRCA which shows that five out of six agencies do not sell the value of what they do. In Chapter One I highlighted the reasons why agencies should shift from a time-based approach to one that focuses on value.

So, why do more than 8 out of 10 agencies not sell according to the value they unlock for clients? In many respects it's a curiosity, because the agencies I talk to all deliver miracles for clients on a daily basis.

DON'T ALLOW YOUR CHOICES TO CONSTRAIN YOUR ABILITY TO SUCCEED

When I look at the value that is being delivered, and ask agency leaders why they don't price based on value, I receive a range of answers, including the ones listed below. I've added a thought under each answer. Some of my answers may at first appear a little glib. But the reality is that every agency has a choice about how it operates. And too often those choices are made automatically, and without thinking. In many cases, what seems to drive agencies to persist with a very ineffective time-based approach is lack of confidence. This lack of confidence is often demonstrated by an anxiety about where the next client will come from.

But if your agency is any good at what it does, you should recognise you will not be constrained by a lack of opportunity in the market. For example, Ibis World[1] estimates that the UK PR and communications market will be worth \$3.4 billion in 2023. The same firm values the US market in 2023 at \$17.8bn.[2] Even the largest agencies are only a tiny fraction of that.

So, if the market isn't the limiting factor, then it is the choices that agency leaders make that causes the inhibitors.

(1) We can't be certain what value we will deliver

- I believe this answer is based on not asking the client the right questions to identify exactly where the agency can contribute value.
  If we think of every client outcome as a destination to be reached, it's possible (and essential) to identify the important steps on the journey to that destination. It's then possible to identify which steps an agency can contribute the most difference to. Your contribution doesn't have to be for every step on the journey.

If you ask the right questions, you can establish where and how you will deliver value. And you can show how you will deliver more value than other options that could be used.

(2) We cannot guarantee results.

- This answer seems to have become embedded in the psyche of PR people. It seems to be based on the view that a PR consultant cannot guarantee what an individual journalist may write, or the action that will be taken by every individual. However, if the right level of research has been carried out, you should be able to guarantee that a well-crafted message will be picked up by the target audiences, and trigger enough of the right response to add value.
  The guarantee doesn't need to be absolute
  As I mentioned in the Introduction, all 'guarantee' means in this context is the ability to show a cause and effect BEFORE work starts. Agencies do not need to guarantee a full outcome like a specific share price valuation, a certain value of sales or winning an election. Pay per click agencies don't guarantee that a client will hit its sales target. They just guarantee that a click will bring a visit.
  What PR agencies can 'guarantee' is that, if their strategy is followed, they will trigger enough of a response from a client's audiences to make a valuable contribution to achieving a desired outcome. The key point here is the need for the agency's strategy to be followed. The client should be hiring you for your expert advice, so don't undermine your expert status by moving away from your strategy. Sometimes clients ask for bad or weak messages to be used. In this scenario an agency has

a choice about whether they accept the client's view or advise a different course of action that stays true to the strategy.

So, I recommend that agencies create a new definition for what guarantee means. It doesn't need to mean the delivery of an absolute result. But it should be related to showing, ahead of time, the impact that the agency's approach will have at key steps on the journey towards an outcome a client values.

(3) **We aren't the only contributor to an outcome**

- You don't have to be the only contributor for your contribution to be valuable.

  As the last answer shows, you don't have to impact every step on a journey. You just need to be able to show where you can make a difference. And if this difference delivers a healthy return on investment for the client, why wouldn't they pay a price that is appropriate for the ROI delivered?

  For example, imagine a client wants help attracting the talent needed to achieve its growth goals. By asking the right questions, you might establish that the client doesn't convert many applicants from interview to a job offer because applicants arrive without fully understanding the needs of the role. And the answers to your questions might also establish that many of those hired decide to leave in the first six months. As a result, you could show the client that you could help to ensure that applicants arrive in the right frame of mind for the role and ensure that they receive a more effective onboarding experience, that is more in line with expectations created by the recruitment process. Both contributions have a clear value. And this value can be quantified by asking other questions about the financial cost of losing people, or the cost of having a low conversion from interview to job offer. This is developed in more detail in Chapter Seven.

So, I recommend that you embrace the fact that you will rarely be the whole solution for a client. And then show them where you contribute the most value – and more value than other options. This will make the cause and effect of working with you much more explicit.

(4) **We've always priced according to time because that's the way the industry does it**

- If someone showed you that you could cut your journey time in half by adopting a simple change in your route, you'd be unlikely to choose to stick to the old route.

You have a choice about how you decide to price your services. And that choice shouldn't be controlled by following the route other people choose – especially if it makes it harder to command a price that the value you deliver deserves.

When you book a flight, you are presented with a range of pricing options. It's the same journey. You arrive at the same destination. So why do some people pay more than others? It's because they assign more value to things like comfort, being able to sleep, better quality food etc. The airline makes this value explicit.

The reality is that time-based pricing has many flaws, and often denies an agency from being paid for the true value it delivers to a client. Until you start to quantify the value you deliver, and make that value explicit, you won't receive the rewards you deserve.

(5) **Clients ask us what our day rate is**

- Tell them you don't price by day rates but by the value you deliver to them. Do you ask your dentist what their day rate is?

  The reality is that clients only ask the day rate question to help assess whether they think they are getting value for money. They do that because agencies don't offer them any other way to assess that value.

This answer obviously begs the question, how do we calculate a value price. I'll cover that in detail in Chapter Seven. But as can be seen from the answer above, it's essential to establish the value of the client outcome you are helping to achieve AND for which of the steps on the journey to that outcome you will contribute the best ROI for a client.

(6) **Procurement insists we provide a rate per day**

- The answer to this question comes back to choices. You can choose to play the procurement game or choose not to. Remember you won't be constrained by lack of opportunity. I've just spoken to an agency owner who was upset that he lost a procurement pitch to a global agency who undercut his price by outsourcing to a freelancer. Why was he upset? I guess because he likes winning. But it's clear that the client was not prepared to pay the price he wanted to charge. So, by choosing an agency that is prepared to get any revenue no matter how low, the client did him a favour.

  I recommend you don't choose to play the procurement game without first establishing your win:loss ratio for procurement lead opportunities. If you win less than 50% of the time, I'd recommend you decline to pursue procurement lead pitches, as the cost of losing will have a significantly negative impact on your agency. We calculate the cost of losing in Chapter Three. If it's higher than 50%, it suggests that you have some kind of edge (are in demand). In this case I'd advise you to have the confidence not to price according to day rates. If you are the frontrunner, they won't reject your approach. If you aren't the frontrunner, then an early rejection will do you a favour.

The role of procurement is to keep out bad choices. They only want to know day rates to drive down price to de-risk a decision that is based on lack of clarity of the value that will be received. If you make the value clear, then the ROI will also be clear.

(7) **The brief we receive doesn't talk about value**

- Accepting a bad brief is a bad choice. If the value for hiring you isn't clear, then it will be very hard to provide a compelling reason why the client should continue to use you.

  I recommend that you ask the client a lot of questions to surface why they want to spend money with your agency, such as:

- What is the outcome they are seeking?

- What is the business value of that outcome?

- When do they want to achieve the outcome?

- What are the financial implications of achieving it early or late?

- What have they done in the past to achieve a similar outcome?

- What is the cost associated with those other routes?

- How successful have the other options been?

- What other things will they be doing to achieve the outcome?

  The answers to questions like these will help you to identify the value that you will be helping to deliver. Crystallising that for a client, and then crystallising how you will be pivotal to success at key steps on the journey, will establish in the client's mind what you should be worth. For example, if an outcome is worth a million dollars and the normal cost of achieving it is half a million dollars, then you will know that the likely ceiling for your fee is half a million dollars. If you want to give the client a pricing advantage by choosing you, then your price will need to be less than half a million dollars. If you calculate that the cost of the time you plan to spend is $100,000, then you can see that there is a potential upside for your price of the gap between $100,000 and perhaps $450,000.

How much of that extra fee you ask for will come down to how
confident you are, how much proof of previous success you have and
how your approach at each of the key steps shows certainty of success.
If you don't surface the value of what the client is trying to achieve, it will be
impossible to prove the value of what you deliver.

(8) **We've had the client for a long time and there isn't a clear goal like there**
     was when we won the account

   • This answer relates to the weakness of the traditional 'retainer' model.
     It shows that the agency thinks it is selling time. Put another way, it
     demonstrates that an agency is only thinking about WHAT they do and
     not WHY they are doing what they do.
     The solution is to ask the client WHY they are hiring your agency.
     What is the outcome they want delivered? The fact that a contract
     relationship is entering its second or tenth year doesn't mean the client
     is devoid of business objectives. It also doesn't mean that the objectives
     have remained the same as at the start of the relationship.
     So, I recommend that you make surfacing client outcomes, and estab-
     lishing the value of achieving them, a key part of the way you do
     business. I recommend you set client expectations that you will do this
     on a quarterly basis, as standard, so that you can be certain that you are
     delivering against their priorities.

If you keep client outcomes and priorities front of mind, you will be able to
link what you do to the achievement of these outcomes. This will enable you to
command a higher price than simply identifying a list of actions.

(9) **There is one long-term goal, and we can't make our fees dependent on**
     achieving that goal

   • It's obvious that you would not want to operate a payment by results
     model when you are not in control over whether the outcome can be
     achieved. But this doesn't mean the client won't pay for the value you
     provide on the journey towards a destination.
     For example, let's say the client's goal is to get a licence to operate. It
     could be to run a lottery or to have a drug approved by the regulator. In
     both these scenarios there is a win-lose event. The client either gets the
     licence, or the approval, or it doesn't. Does that mean the client won't
     spend a lot trying to achieve the outcome or won't pay for help on the
     journey? Of course not. The client will calculate how much they are
     prepared to risk to give themselves a chance of winning. They have no

absolute guarantee of success. So, what defines the price to be paid for your help in trying to achieve the outcome? Is it the time it takes or is it the difference your expertise makes at important steps on the journey to the outcome?

One agency I trained said they had charged a client £200,000 to help achieve approval for a vaccine. That sounds like a decent fee. But, since that vaccine achieved approval, the pharma company concerned has generated £2 billion. The agency was not the only contributor to achieving the approval, but it was pivotal to creating the right mindset for the various stakeholders that were part of the approval process. So, could/should the agency have charged more? There is no magic algorithm to use. But if, in advance, they had established how pivotal they would be to success at key steps on the journey, they may have been able to command a higher price. In Chapter Four we explore how you can increase the perceived certainty of success with a branded methodology or HOW.

Don't let the lack of an absolute guarantee of success persuade you to charge a lower price than your contribution deserves. Understand how much the client is risking to achieve a goal and charge according to the importance of your contribution to achieving it.

(10)   We don't want to get caught on payment by results

- By now, based on the answers above, you will no doubt recognise that selling according to the value you deliver does not mean you have to wait until an outcome has been achieved to be paid.

  Do clients expect their employees to wait to be paid until an outcome has been achieved? Obviously not? They calculate how much money they are prepared to put at risk in their efforts to achieve the outcome. Then they put a team together to achieve that outcome. They pay each member of the team for their contribution to trying to achieve the outcome.

  Therefore, the chosen agency needs to establish the value of their contribution to the 'team'. The value won't be the time the agency spends, but the outputs and outcomes of the expertise of the people doing the work.

  You can use a time-based calculation to establish a minimum price, and then assess how much of a premium should be added to the importance of your contribution to the team. To use a football (soccer) analogy, if you need to score to win, the team member who commands the biggest premium is likely to be the striker. Stopping people scoring has a value. Creating opportunities to score has a value. Having the proven ability to do these things increases the price people are prepared to pay.

There is, of course, no reason why you couldn't offer the client pricing options. One option could be a premium priced fee regardless of the outcome. Another option could be a slightly lower fee topped up by a success fee. The second option would cost more. In my experience, most clients tend to select the certainty of the first option rather than what they perceive as a price penalty for success.

The secret to successful value-based pricing is surfacing WHY clients are prepared to invest their money with your agency, i.e. establishing the business value they expect to receive.

CHECKLIST

(1) Have you identified the business outcome the client is hiring you to help deliver?

(2) Have you quantified the business/financial value to the client of achieving that outcome?

(3) Have you identified the important steps to be taken to achieve that outcome?

(4) Have you identified what value you contribute at each of those steps?

(5) Have you established the importance of your contribution to each of those steps, as compared to other potential contributors? If you show a better return, the client will choose you.

(6) Have you captured proof of the value you have delivered for this client, and other clients, so you can create a sense of certainty that the value will be delivered if the client chooses you?

(7) Do you practice self-acknowledgement about the value you deliver, so you build confidence and belief in your ability to command a premium price?

(8) Do you have an explicit way of doing things that makes the delivery of the value the client expects more certain?

You can find a downloadable list of questions to ask at www.onva.co.uk/sellingvalue.

3

THE IMPORTANCE OF BEING 'MARMITE[1] NOT VANILLA'

Marmite[2] is a British savoury food spread. It's based on yeast extract and is a by-product of brewing. It's manufactured by Unilever and has a very particular flavour that not everybody likes. So, Unilever has developed a long-lasting marketing campaign that gets consumers to make a binary choice – to either love or hate Marmite.

To create 'haters' may seem like a strange marketing strategy. But it is in fact incredibly smart. Because Unilever recognised that not everyone will like Marmite, it hasn't wasted its effort trying to appeal to everyone – only to find that it has disappointed people with its promises. Instead, it has made it clear that there is a very specific group of people who will enjoy the product – the lovers. And in doing so, Unilever has created a cult following for Marmite.

Most agencies follow a very different strategy. They present themselves a bit like vanilla ice cream. It's very hard to distinguish one vanilla ice cream from another. There may be subtle taste differences, but ultimately if you put 20 bowls of different vanilla ice creams side by side, it would be very hard to identify one brand from another.

But that's what most agencies do. They define themselves by describing WHAT they do, not WHY or HOW they do it. Here is a list of nine agency descriptions picked at random from website visits. I've removed the agency names.

(1) At Vanilla, we've mastered the art of communications over 20 years.

(2) A leading tech and fintech PR agency working with startups and global brands.

(3) We're an integrated PR and social agency based in London and New York.

(4) We are an award-winning consumer and charity public relations agency and specialise in celebrity engagement.

(5) A close-knit team of journalists, media specialists and PR experts.

(6) We are an independent creative digital marketing and communications agency based in London.

(7) Vanilla is a full-service PR and communications agency.

(8) Vanilla PR is a London based Fashion PR and Communications Agency that offers a range of services including Public Relations, Digital Services and Social Media Management.

(9) A London-based media and communications consultancy specialising in Beauty PR and Health and Wellness PR.

Does a vanilla description make them a bad agency? Absolutely not. In fact, although I don't know many of these agencies personally, I'm sure they all do great work that delivers value to clients. When I looked at their websites they just didn't explain explicitly WHY or HOW they do it.

And that's the tragedy of not making the value you deliver explicit.

If you were a client on the hunt for an agency that could help you achieve important business outcomes, would the descriptions above make it clear who could help you best? The answer is no. The sector specialisations might rule some in, or some out, but none would give you that Marmite response that you are going to love them.

So, what would you most likely do? You'd do what most clients do when confronted with the same challenge – you'd put together a beauty parade to see if one of the agencies stands out from the others when you meet them.

This makes agency selection incredibly expensive for the client and incredibly costly for the agencies.

THE COST OF NOT MAKING YOUR VALUE EXPLICIT

Do you know what the average cost of a complex pitch is to your agency? That's a pitch that needs ideas creating, a proposal writing, a deck created, pitch rehearsals and maybe two or more rounds of presentations if you get to the shortlist.

If you do know the cost, then you are in the significant minority.

Losing is seen as a cost of doing business. And, because the cost of LOSING isn't front of mind, agencies lose more often than they should.

Every time I train agencies, I ask them what their win rate is. The answers range from 10% to 80%. But at least 80% of agencies fall into the 10%–40% bracket. This means most are losing between six and nine of every 10 pitches! That level of failure is usually justified by the value of the pitches that are won.

So, what is the cost of a lost pitch?

Obviously, this will vary by agency, their individual charge rates, and how much effort they typically put in to trying to win.

In Chart 3 below, you will see an assessment of the time taken by different people in the pitch process – and what this adds up to in both time and money.

This example shows that 28 days of people's time is expended – in other words almost one and a half months of time! And the cost – based on the charge rates – is £25,220. If you lose 10 pitches a year, that is a quarter of a million in lost fees and 280 days of wasted time. That's 1.4 billable years (on the assumption people have 200 days to bill).

Imagine what you could do with that time to transform the performance of your agency.

One agency I spoke to recently admitted that they had lost 53 pitches last year. That equates to £1.33 million in lost billing and 1,503 days or 7.5 billable years! Why did they lose so many? It's not because they aren't a good agency – they are. And it's not because they can't win pitches – they do. In fact, last year they had their best year ever. It was because the pitches they lost were pitches they had little chance of winning, because they didn't make their WHY and HOW explicit before the client invited them to pitch. We look at the importance of a compelling WHY in Chapter Three.

This lack of clarity about WHY they exist, and therefore who they can satisfy best, is unhelpful in two ways:

- It means clients invite them to a pitch without believing they can deliver the required outcome.

- It means the agency hasn't an effective way to sift prospects based on what the agency believes.

Time wasted by losing pitches						
Hours per person per pitch						
Team Role	**AE**	**AM**	**SAM**	**AD**	**Director**	**TOTAL**
Brief and qualification	-	4	-	4	2	10
Brainstorm and campaign idea development	10	10	10	10	4	44
Research	5	5	-	3	-	13
Proposal and deck prep - 3 rounds including procurement	20	20	20	20	12	92
Pricing	5	-	-	4	2	11
Proofing	4	-	4	4	-	12
Rehearsal	3	3	3	3	3	15
Presentation including travel - 2 rounds	6	6	6	6	6	30
Total hours	**53**	**48**	**43**	**54**	**29**	**227**

	AE	AM	SAM	AD	Director	TOTAL
Hour per complex pitch	53	48	43	54	29	227
Cost of hours in billable time	£60	£80	£100	£150	£200	
Total cost	**£3,180**	**£3,840**	**£4,300**	**£8,100**	**£5,800**	**£25,220**

Average cost of each lost pitch	**£25,220**
Average days lost per pitch	**28.38**

Number of pitches	Billings lost	Days lost	Years lost
3	£75,660	85.13	0.43
5	£126,100	141.88	0.71
8	£201,760	227.00	1.14
12	£302,640	340.50	1.70
15	£378,300	425.63	2.13
18	£453,960	510.75	2.55
20	£504,400	567.50	2.84

£504,400 lost billings for 20 lost pitches
2.84 years lost losing 20 pitches

©Crispin Manners

Source: Author's original work.

Chart 3. Cost of a Complex Pitch – Time Wasted by Losing Pitches.

As you can see, if they hadn't wasted 1,503 days losing pitches, then they could have spent more time transforming the performance of their agency:

- Developing their people – and thus freeing the senior team to spend more time working ON the business not IN the business.

- Selling back the value of what they deliver – thus creating a more resilient and loyal client base.

- Innovating new services – thus being more compelling to changing needs.

- Changing the way they deliver existing services – such as changing meeting practices mentioned in Chapter One – thus delivering more value from less effort.

And their people could have gone home on time – thus making the employee experience less stressful.

WHAT'S STOPPING AGENCIES USING THE MARMITE FACTOR?

Why do agencies describe themselves as purveyors of activities rather than enablers of outcomes of value?

The answer seems to be based on the fear that if they appear to be pistachio rather than vanilla, they will be attractive to fewer organisations and therefore miss out on growth opportunities. To use the Marmite analogy, they are afraid they will create a 'hater' on arrival. But this ignores the other Marmite option, that they will create a 'lover' on arrival. If like me, you love pistachio ice cream, you will instantly be more attracted by the promise of pistachio than the promise of vanilla.

And, as the Introduction explains, most agencies revenue aspirations are tiny in relation to the size of the PR market.

So, there is no need to be fearful based on the availability of work. Instead, you should be fearful of not making your agency as attractive as you can to the clients you can satisfy best.

WHAT DOES A COMPELLING WHY LOOK LIKE?

At the heart of a compelling WHY, or PURPOSE, is BELIEF. This should be based on what you believe is the difference you want to make, because it will be this belief that keeps your agency moving forward.

So, a compelling WHY should capture the reason your agency exists – the difference you want the agency to make.

A good WHY can be expressed by what I call an 'I believe' statement. If you think of the apocryphal President Kennedy story about the cleaner at Cape Canaveral, he said: '*I believe I am helping to put a man on the moon*'.

If asked, what do you want your people to say they believe they are helping to do? I'm sure it is likely to be more than: '*I believe I am helping to get press coverage*'. There just isn't enough value in that to sustain an employee's interest and loyalty, or attract a client.

The message or WHY statement you should try to surface, should:

(1) Crystallise the value that you deliver to clients.

(2) Attract clients who believe what you believe.

(3) Attract employees who believe what you believe.

(4) Easily convert into an 'I believe' statement.

(5) Provide the foundation for a highly differentiated HOW that sets you apart from your competitors AND commands a premium price that transforms your profitability.

(6) Show that your agency is a force for good.

- This last point is often the subject of debate with agency owners. I've heard many times expressions like: *We help get press coverage not create a cure for cancer*. That's true. But the reason you do what you do inevitably, and inexorably, leads to one outcome or another. And you have a choice whether or not this high-level outcome is a force for good. The reason why it is important to be seen as a force for good is that clients are now expected, by their various stakeholders, to show how they are a force for good AND many people want to feel that the work they do has some purpose. So, if you want to attract and retain the best clients and people, you need the outcome of your work to be seen as a force for good.

Here are some WHY statements that are being used by PR agencies. I've made some comments about each which shows how a WHY, which is compelling to organisations and people with very specific beliefs and needs, drives success.

(1) **We make positive change happen**[3] (by partnering with game changers who have ambitious ideas and solutions for a sustainable future).

- This agency is a force for good because they are helping their clients make a difference to creating a sustainable future. With an explicit WHY like this, it's no surprise that they helped multiple clients at COP27 – companies that shared their belief about making positive change happen.

(2) **We are on a mission to make people healthier and happier**[4] (through life-changing education and communications).

  - This agency is a force for good in a way that resonates with their people as this quote from an account manager shows: 'One of the highlights for me last year was receiving an email from a HIV positive man saying our campaign has changed his life and that his involvement was one of his greatest achievements'.

(3) **We make lives more playful.**[5]

  - With an explicit WHY like this, it's not surprising that they represent some of the world's biggest and best toy brands. Because of the compelling nature of the WHY, this agency grew by 53% during the pandemic.

(4) **We deliver change that makes Ireland and the world a better place.**[6]

  - This WHY is appealing to organisations that want to deliver change. It should therefore be no surprise that this agency has helped to deliver some transformational changes in Ireland such as the enactment of the Gender Pay Gap Information Act.

So, make sure you are explicit about what you believe, and it will be a magnet for people who believe it too.

HOW DO I MAKE MY AGENCY'S WHY EXPLICIT?

One of the things I've found when helping agency leaders to crystallise their WHY and HOW, is that they are often so focused on their day-to-day actions that they are 'blind' to the value they deliver to clients.

Identify What You Believe

So, to open their eyes to just how valuable they really are, I take the owners of the agency right back to three essential components of success:

(1) **Their personal beliefs and passions.**

- When these are identified, it's uncanny how they are embedded in the way the agency operates. The problem is that it's usually done implicitly rather than explicitly.

(2) **The difference they make that they'd like to be remembered for.**

- Most agency owners I talk to have relatively small egos and haven't seen their 'legacy' as being important. However, when they think about the question, we soon surface some important factors which impact on the way the agency operates. For example, one agency owner I have helped said he would like to be remembered as someone who helped people realise that they had the power to have a positive impact on others. The moment he said this he realised that it was exactly the value he was trying to deliver with his agency.

(3) **The things that energise them.**

- Agency owners are always capable people. And, as a result of being capable, they end up doing many things that drain their energy, rather than things that energise them. As the primary energy source for the agency, it makes no sense to do things that inhibit your ability to operate at your best. By identifying your primary sources of energy, you will be able to define HOW you deliver value to clients in a way that keeps you energised.

The answers to these questions create a foundation for the agency WHY because the answers surface what the leaders(s) of the agency believe in.

Identify the Clients that Energise You Most

The next step is to identify which clients energise you and why. When I did this recently with an agency leader in the United States, we soon realised that the clients the owner was most energised by were those who wanted to make a positive impact on people's lives. This covered a big range of organisations from meat producers to toy companies and an irrigation/water management company. This soon translated into this WHY. *We deliver a positive impact on people, the community, and the world.*

We also identified that these clients were innovators, providers of a new and smarter way of doing things and, organisations that recognised that to drive a change in behaviour, they would need ideas with real cut-through. Not only did this help to identify who the agency satisfies best, but also identified some key elements of HOW they do it.

Another example of making your WHY more explicit is the toy and games specialist I mentioned above. The CEO came on a course I deliver for the PRCA on how to manage an agency.[7]

At the time of the training, the reason for clients to engage them was expressed on the website in a vanilla format: *Creativity, knowledge and teamwork are three things that clients talk about when they use us.*

Two weeks after the training the website said: *We are a PR agency on a mission to make the world a more playful place.* This delivered an immediate return. A prospect who had been recommended to use the agency, said she wasn't planning to do so because she felt they would be too small for her needs, but had visited the website and decided, on the strength of the WHY statement, that she wanted to work with them because they shared the same purpose. This translated into a contract without the need to pitch.

When I started to help the agency, the CEO and her team realised that the difference they wanted to make was to people and not to the world. So, the WHY became: *We make lives more playful.* And, as we worked on shaping HOW they deliver that value, the impact on people became more obvious. As a result, the WHY can be extended to make the impact on people even more explicit: *We make lives more playful by connecting consumers of every age with brands that help people learn to play, learn through play, and unleash the transformative power of play.*

This can be said another way: *'I believe I'm helping to make lives more playful by connecting consumers of every age with brands that help people learn to play, learn through play, and unleash the transformative power of play.'*

Don't limit your WHY if some of your current clients don't believe what you believe – you can always replace them. Instead, be inspired by the ability to attract clients that share your belief. Being more compelling to people who want to make the same difference as you will be the energy source that powers your agency forward.

CHECKLIST

(1) Have you calculated the cost of a complex pitch?

(2) Have you calculated the cost of losing, and used this as a motivator to surface the value you deliver to clients?

(3) Have you identified what you believe in as the foundation for the value you want your agency to deliver?

(4) Have you identified the clients, and the work, that energises you most – and why that is the case?

(5) Have you captured your WHY in an 'I believe' statement that would resonate with your people and your clients?

(6) Have you tested your WHY by asking: 'why does that matter' until you reach the highest level of value possible.

4

WHY IT'S IMPORTANT TO EXPLAIN HOW VALUE IS DELIVERED IN A WAY THAT IS UNIQUE TO YOUR AGENCY

The last chapter described why it is essential to make the value your agency delivers – your WHY – explicit. This is the message that shows clients, and people, WHY you would be a good choice. It gives you a distinct advantage over vanilla agencies.

But, even if a client shares your Purpose, they will still need convincing that you are the best choice. This means that you will need to show them you have a proven way of delivering the OUTCOME they want. And, just as your WHY needs to be explicit, your HOW does too.

In this chapter we will look at:

- The need to ensure that your HOW is explicit.

- The need to ensure that you use every opportunity to bring your HOW, and the business value it delivers, to life – such as through case studies.

- The need to ensure that your HOW is unique to you.

ENSURE THAT YOU MAKE YOUR HOW EXPLICIT

Most agencies just talk about WHAT they do rather than HOW they do it. The examples below come from the websites of PR agencies. They help to demonstrate the difference between implicit and explicit approaches.

(1) We help ethical organisations increase profile, revenue, customers and footfall.

   Our[1] work is proven to raise profiles, attract investment, increase footfall and ultimately boost revenue for the clients we have the privilege to work with.

   We:

   • Provide strategic marketing and public relations services.

   • Provide event management.

   • Are Google-accredited in digital marketing services.

      – This agency has really thought about their WHY and it comes through strongly on their website. *We help ethical organisations increase profile, revenue, customers and footfall.*

      – So, if I was a client, I'd be interested. But they leap from an excellent WHY to WHAT they do, **not** HOW they do it. If they add a powerful HOW, they would be even more compelling to the ethical organisations they want to attract.

(2) Digital[2] PR, SEO & Content agency, proudly delivering campaigns that are: Data and audience-led; Creative and engaging; Results-driven. We're a digital marketing agency that love to evolve conventional marketing models into effective, measurable integrated strategies that deliver impactful results for our clients. Our unique 'Creative Intelligence®' approach is centred around the functions of the brain – left brain (data and intelligence) and right brain (creativity and content).

   • This agency is interesting because the first thing you see is a list of WHAT they do, not WHY they do it. They then have a general reference to results which is OK but not differentiated. However, they then refer to a unique approach – their HOW – with a registered name. This clearly differentiates them from a host of other Digital PR, SEO & Content agencies, of which there are thousands.

      If this explicit HOW was married to an explicit WHY, the agency would have a much better chance of winning the clients it can satisfy best.

(3) We[3] deliver change that makes Ireland and the world a better place. In our work, we use our unique CHANGE methodology, which has been

developed and honed over the past decade, contributing to some of the most transformational changes in Irish society.

- This description combines an explicit WHY with an explicit HOW. It shows there is a method used (which is explained further on the website) to deliver transformational change. And this gives clients confidence that hiring this agency won't be a big gamble.

You need to connect your HOW with your WHY in a way that increases client confidence and belief that you will deliver the outcomes they want.

ENSURE YOUR CASE STUDIES BRING YOUR HOW, AND THE VALUE DELIVERED TO CLIENTS, TO LIFE

Most agencies include case studies on their website to prove that they can deliver value to clients. But, while case studies are there to build belief that the agency is a safe buy, most fail to do that because they focus on WHAT was done rather than WHY (the value/outcome the work delivered) or HOW (the unique approach that made the outcome more certain).

Most case studies are written to satisfy people who are called USER BUYERS. While it's important to include information that is seen as important by user buyers, it's VITAL to include information that is seen as ESSENTIAL by ECONOMIC BUYERS.

Economic buyers and user buyers are explained in more detail in Chapter Eleven. But the critical difference between the two is that economic buyers **create** budgets to deliver BUSINESS OUTCOMES and user buyers **spend** budgets to deliver OUTPUTS THEY CAN COUNT.

The extracts from the case study below are an adaptation from an example I saw on a website. I could have chosen a thousand others that are written in the same way. I'm using it as an example to show how the value of the work – which looks very good, and I'm certain delivered huge value to the client – is undersold.

My aim is not to be critical of what the agency did, but to show how a focus on value could have produced a very different case study that made the WHY and HOW explicit. In short, the agency could have brought the huge value they undoubtedly delivered into sharp focus – thus making them much more attractive to future clients AND the client concerned.

Heading: Engaging with theme park fans through Digital PR.

This heading describes WHAT was done not WHY it was done. The heading implies that value was delivered but doesn't say what that was. It therefore makes it harder for an economic buyer to understand the return on investment (**ROI**) that the client received.

Objectives: We were asked to secure more online media coverage that showed visitors would have 'amazing memories.'

The objective is expressed in a way that is OUTPUT not OUTCOME focused. It was probably written by a user buyer. Agencies use the term ROI all the time. But the way they define it – in terms of outputs – shows that they don't see the money a client spends with them as a true investment. In this example, if the client is spending £xxx (I don't know what the budget was), the expected ROI is unlikely to be online coverage. **The client can't bank online coverage.**

So, let's ask the 'why does that matter' question to surface the business reason why the client is investing money in PR – the business OUTCOME that the economic buyer sees as the ROI expected from the investment in PR.

Q: Why did the client hire this agency?
A: To secure more online media coverage.

Q: Why does that matter?
A: Because it increases awareness of the client?

Q: Why does that matter?
A: Because it will help them get noticed by potential customers.

Q: Why does that matter?
A: Because they need to sell more tickets.

Q: Why does that matter?
A: Because if they don't sell more tickets, they will miss their revenue and profit targets.

Q: Why does that matter?
A: Because if they miss their revenue and profit targets, they will not be able to invest in new attractions.

Q: Why does that matter?
A: Because if they are not able to bring their new attractions to market, they will become less compelling to consumers and may go out of business.

In this example, the highest level of value is staying in business. And when you consider that this campaign took place when the cost-of-living crisis, caused by high inflation, was beginning to bite, then the risk of missing revenue and going out of business was probably front-of-mind for the CEO of the client.

It's unlikely that the client would express the brief as to 'help us stay in business' but it could be to 'help us sell more tickets.'

So, if this was your agency, what's the moral of this case study so far, if you want to be properly rewarded for the value you deliver?

(1) **You must not accept a WHAT level brief. You need to convert it into a WHY level brief.**
    We discuss how to do that in Chapter Seven. The first thing to do is to use the 'why does that matter' question to bring the highest level of value to the fore. If you don't surface the business OUTCOME it will be very hard, if not impossible, to charge a value-based price.

(2) **You need to quantify how the expected business ROI will be measured.**
    Let's assume in this case it is ticket sales. You will need to ask questions about ticket sales to define what your contribution to sales is expected to be. If you don't define your contribution, it will be very hard, if not impossible, to charge a value-based price.

(3) **You will need to ask the client to share sales data, so you can show the impact you are having on sales.** If you don't get the client to share essential data, it will be very hard, if not impossible, to charge a value-based price. How to do this is covered in Chapter Eight.

What We Did

Our strategy focused on leveraging theme park fans and influencers to raise the profile of the park. We sourced unique data to share with the media. We used our strong media relationships to secure coverage for the client's biggest events.

As you can see, the description above is no doubt a good strategy but it uses words that hundreds of other agencies use – *leveraging fans and influencers...* *strong media relationships etc.*

It doesn't show explicitly that there is a method being followed. For example, what does the agency do to:

• Source unique data.

• Build *strong media relationships* so that then can be used to a client's advantage.

If you use many of the same approaches as other agencies (which will inevitably be the case), then you need to show you have a unique method for increasing the certainty that the desired outputs and outcomes will be delivered.

To enable you to identify the value you will deliver, and be able to price for that contribution, you should not accept a WHAT level brief. You must convert it into a WHY level brief.

Results

xxx pieces of online coverage over a 5-month period.

xx links with an average Domain Authority of xx.

xx national hits.

xx pieces of additional print coverage.

xxx billion reach.

The actual numbers shared were very impressive. They address the objective of securing more online media coverage. But they don't address the need to reinforce that visitors have 'amazing memories.' It's implied this happened, but it should be explicit.

More importantly, they count outputs in a way that may satisfy a user buyer but would not satisfy an economic buyer.

Imagine the CEO (economic buyer) asks: *'What did we get for the money we spent with that PR agency'*? And the client's PR manager (user buyer) says: *'We got a lot of great coverage in the national press'*. The CEO is most likely to ask: *'What did the coverage achieve for the business?* And, if the PR manager can't give an answer that contains business value, the CEO is likely to be dissatisfied with the PR Manager and the agency. In buoyant markets, this may not become a problem. But in tough markets it could become a real problem for the PR manager and the agency.

If the sales OUTCOME had been surfaced, and data shared to prove the agency's contribution, the results might look something like this:

Results aimed at the Economic buyer

xx% increase in visitors to the website.

xx% increase in the visits to the ticket portal.

xx% increase in tickets sold.

xx% increase in tickets sold without affiliate fees (thus making the tickets more profitable). This result addresses a way that your agency can show a better ROI than say a marketing campaign with an affiliate. If you do this, then the client could be persuaded to move the budget from another method of driving ticket sales over to you.

Results aimed at the User buyer

xxx pieces of online coverage over a 5-month period.

xx% increase in online coverage with links.

xx% increase in high spending visitors that click links (Would need to know the visitor demographic that spends more).

xx national hits.

Don't leave the value you deliver buried under a list of user buyer focused OUTPUTS. Always ensure that you identify your contribution to the economic buyer's OUTCOME.

WHY YOU NEED A BRANDED METHODOLOGY

In the sections above I've referred to the need to have a HOW that is unique to you – a branded methodology.

When I raise the subject of branded methodologies with agency owners, I'm quite often met with statements like: *We are a PR agency not a management consultancy.*

That is of course true. But remember you have complete freedom of choice over how you make the contribution you provide more explicit.

If your contribution is significant, then it makes sense to describe your contribution in a way that can command a premium price.

To bring this to life, I am going to use a management consultancy example. I will show how smart that consultancy was to create an approach that targeted economic buyer needs. I will also show how they did it in a way that was simple, visual, and made the value they contributed completely explicit. As a result, they built the buyer's belief and confidence that their approach would pay off. And they correctly set the buyer's expectations about the value that would be delivered.

The consultancy I am talking about is Boston Consulting Group (BCG). They are a premier league global management consultancy. Although they are very good, they have very good competitors like Bain and McKinsey. So, just as with PR agencies, clients have a choice about who they choose. So, what was a differentiator that set BCG apart? One answer is a branded method-ology called the Growth Share Matrix (BCG Matrix). If you want to learn more about BCG's Matrix, I have included a link to a helpful article and video in the footnote.[4]

BCG made itself indispensable to Fortune 500 companies in the 1970s and 1980s by creating the Growth Share Matrix. What's significant about the timing is that the 1970s was the last time we had a period of 'stagflation' – a combination of high inflation and low growth. So, BCG was addressing the same challenges that PR agencies face today – how to win client confidence and belief in a period of significant uncertainty.

When certainty is in short supply, business leaders know that their success will be defined by the quality of the decisions they make. To de-risk their decisions, they often turn to EXPERTS to help guide them.

The study I mentioned in the Introduction reinforces the need to make the right choices when it comes to what to cut and what to invest in. The BCG Matrix was designed to help with those decisions. It was designed to help clients to decide which parts of their business no longer delivered a healthy ROI and which delivered the cash (cash cows) they needed to fund the future growth stars. It enabled clients to take a *'progressive'* approach by deciding what to cut and where to invest. Smart leaders know that 'weathering the storm' isn't enough, it's also important to build the growth engines of the future. They know that they need to focus on priorities rather than spread investment and action too thinly.

So, BCG created the BCG Matrix to meet the fundamental need to de-risk decisions and identify priorities. In short, BCG met the economic buyer's need for increased CERTAINTY.

MAKING YOUR METHODOLOGY A VISUAL TOOL

Part of the brilliance of the BCG Matrix is that it turned a very complex topic into something that could be addressed by a very simple visual tool – a four quadrant grid! It helped clients define their investment landscape and then make business critical decisions (Chart 4).[5]

BCG used the BCG Matrix to not only prove their EXPERT capability but also show clients the journey they would have to travel to reach their

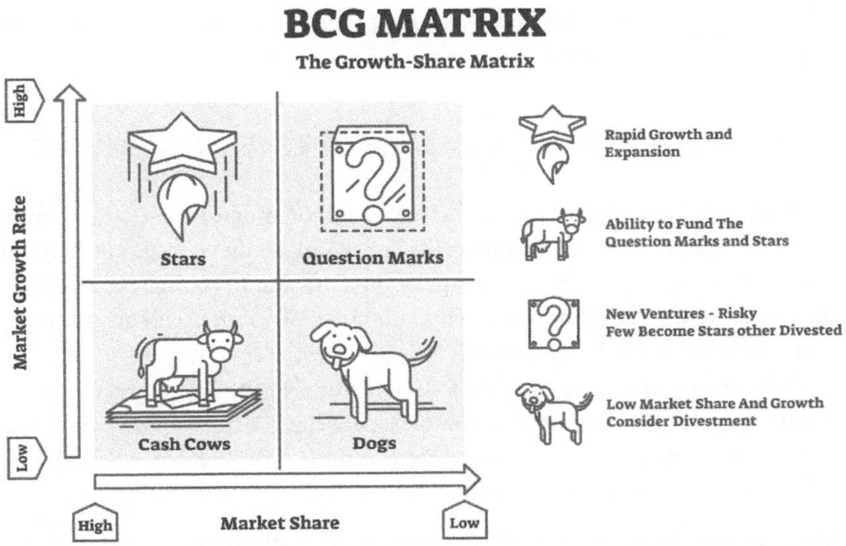

BCG MATRIX

The Growth-Share Matrix

Chart 4. The BCG (Boston Consulting Group) Growth Share Matrix.

destination. At the height of the Growth Share Matrix's success, it was used by about half of all Fortune 500 companies.

WHAT CAN PR AGENCIES LEARN FROM THE BCG MATRIX?

(1) Clients run towards EXPERTS in a period of uncertainty.

(2) Clients value a service that reduces the risk of their decisions – makes OUTCOMES more CERTAIN.

(3) Clients will invest in a service that helps them increase their ROI.

(4) VISUAL tools can be very persuasive by SIMPLIFYING complex topics.

(5) Visual tools that help clients PRIORITISE are very valuable. In Chapter Five we give some examples that can be used by agencies to do just that.

To summarise, your agency will be much more compelling to clients if you have a unique methodology that helps focus action on business priorities and increases the CERTAINTY of achieving desired business OUTCOMES. By doing so you will reinforce your EXPERT status and increase client confidence and belief in your approach. This will enable you to command a premium over lesser agencies who do not satisfy the need for certainty.

AN EXAMPLE FROM THE WORLD OF EMPLOYEE ENGAGEMENT

To bring methodologies back to the world of communications, let's look at Inspiring Workplaces Consulting (IWC).[6] IWC is the consulting arm of Inspiring Workplaces Group, a company on a mission *to change the world by transforming the world of work.* This is a clear WHY that will attract organisations who share that purpose.

IWC defines this transformation as: Creating People-First organisations. Becoming truly people-first is a complex challenge, so to simplify the challenge, and to help clients prioritise their action, IWC created a visual tool (Chart 5) – the PeopleFirst Matrix (PFM).

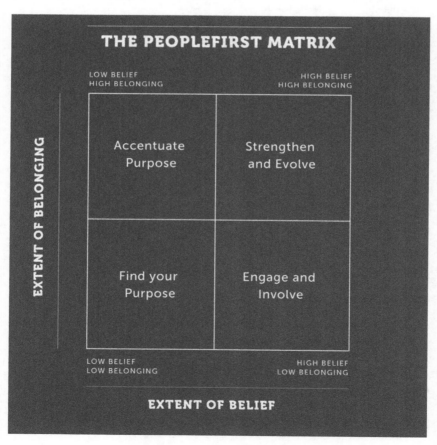

Chart 5. Inspiring Workplaces Consulting People-First Matrix.

As you can see from Chart 5, IWC has shown that the route to becoming people-first can be charted by building BELIEF and BELONGING. And it has created a service using a diagnostic tool, to position clients on the PFM which helps clients identify where they are on their journey to becoming people-first.

To help clients to prioritise the action they need to take, IWC has created a methodology called COMPASS.

COMPASS breaks the journey into six components – see Chart 6.

(1) Inspiring purpose and culture.

(2) Inspiring leadership and communication.

(3) Inclusion and community.

(4) Society and sustainability.

(5) Wellbeing.

(6) Employee VOICE.

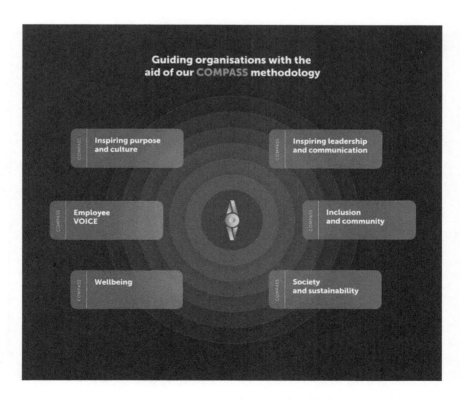

Chart 6. Inspiring Workplaces Consulting's COMPASS Methodology.

This enables IWC consultants to agree which of the six areas the client needs to focus on to reach their destination.

It helps clients to create an integrated people-first strategy, with the six COMPASS components working together, rather than pursuing a series of disconnected initiatives aimed at improving the employee experience. And it builds buyer confidence and belief that IWC will help them become people-first with greater CERTAINTY and speed.

HOW TO SURFACE THE STEPS IN YOUR APPROACH TO DELIVERING CLIENT SUCCESS

There are many different ways that you can identify the key components of your method. IWC did this by analysing a decade's award-winning entries to the Inspiring Workplace Awards. You could do it by analysing your best work – something I help agencies do all the time.

You could run your own HOW workshop as follows:

(1) Identify at least three client campaigns about which you are most proud.

(2) Identify the value you delivered to the client – not just OUTPUTS but OUTCOMES. Make these outputs and outcomes very explicit and granular.

(3) Then look at HOW you delivered those outputs and outcomes.

(4) Identify anything that appears across all the examples – as these will be the foundation for the steps in your method.

(5) Make each step you identify unique to you.

- For example, if you identify that you are great at telling client stories, don't make storytelling one of the components of your method, because hundreds of other agencies will say that too. Instead, identify the way you surface a client's best story and make this your unique approach.

(6) Identify at least three examples of work that did not deliver client value and then work out why.

- It's highly likely that the client did not share your purpose – your WHY.

- It's also likely that you did not follow the same approach that you used for your most successful work.

If you don't make it easy for clients to see you as an EXPERT, and reinforce that expert status with a method that satisfies the need for certainty, you will find it hard to be rewarded for the value you deliver.

CHECKLIST

(1) Does your approach focus on delivering business OUTCOMES and not just communications OUTPUTS?

(2) Have you brought the approach you use to the surface, and packaged it as a methodology?

(3) Have you checked that you aren't describing your approach in the language other agencies use?

(4) Have you given your method a name – so that you can accentuate your expert status by promoting the power of your branded method?

(5) Does your HOW link to your WHY, and build confidence and belief in your ability to deliver your WHY?

(6) Have you brought your method to life by embedding it in existing case studies?

(7) Have you identified the clients, and the work, that energises you most – and why that is the case?

(8) Does your HOW increase CERTAINTY for the client?

(9) Does your HOW help the client to PRIORITISE action?

(10) Have you captured your HOW in simple, visual tools?

5

HOW TO CREATE THE TOOLS THAT BRING YOUR BRANDED METHOD TO LIFE AND GIVE YOUR TEAM WAYS TO REINFORCE IT

In Chapter Four, we identified why it's important to have a differentiated method for delivering OUTPUTS and OUTCOMES to clients.

It is clear from my work with agencies around the world that the leaders often find it hard to translate a clear WHY and HOW into processes that they can use each day to reinforce the value that they deliver. This is because they are so focused on WHAT they do, that they rarely identify HOW they do it.

The previous chapter outlined an approach to identify the steps in your implicit approach and embed these in an explicit branded methodology. Now we will look at how you can bring these steps to life with visual tools that help you to engage the client and your team with your method. This will enable them to have a personal experience of your EXPERT approach.

Let's look at elements many agencies assign to their approach. And let's see how you can avoid the trap of describing what you do in a way that makes it sound the same as many other agencies.

TOOLS TO APPEAR MORE EXPERT AND MORE DIFFERENT

Excellent Media/Audience/Influencer Relationships

Many agencies claim that they have excellent relationships, and that these relationships give their clients an edge. However, while agencies present this as an advantage, clients will see it as a basic requirement – they expect you to have nurtured great relationships.

So one way you can differentiate your agency is to show how you select/ prioritise the organisations or individuals that you plan to target on the client's behalf. You can create a visual tool to do this, and engage the client in the prioritisation process – see Chart 7. By using a visual tool in this way, you can turn the production of a media list (which is assumed as a low value exercise carried out by junior staff) into a high value consulting opportunity which has prioritisation at its heart.

Chart 7 does the following:

(1) It lists the most obvious people/organisations (outlets) to target – some of which may be provided by your client.

(2) It identifies the level of influence the outlet has over the client's target audiences. For example, if you were trying to influence nurses in the United Kingdom, the Royal College of Nursing would have very high levels of influence.

   - You could identify this position in a workshop with the client based on your combined knowledge of the outlet concerned. In some cases, a client may know more about an outlet than you and vice versa, so it is good to pool knowledge to get a shared commitment to why the outlet is important. This can accentuate your expert knowledge.

(3) It identifies the level of interest each outlet has in the client's topic.

   - As with the level of influence above, you could identify/agree this in a workshop with a client – thus demonstrating your expert knowledge.

Once the positions are fixed on the spider graph, you can use the positions to help explain why you will follow a specific strategy to ensure your effort is focused on delivering the best ROI for the client.

For example, you could recommend the following prioritisation of outlets:

(1) Media 5 would be your top target because it has the joint highest level of influence and very high interest. Because of the high level of interest, you wouldn't need to work too hard to take advantage of their influence.

   - You'd probably treat Influencer 10 in the same way.

(2) Media 6 would be your second target because it has the joint highest levels of influence. However, because its interest is lower, you'd be recommending a targeted strategy to get the level of interest up.

   - You'd probably treat Organisation 3 in the same way.

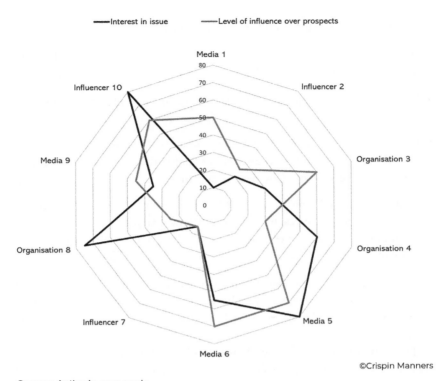

Source: Author's own work.

Chart 7. Prioritising Sources of Influence.

(3) Although Influencer 2 and Organisation 8 have the same low level of influence, you'd probably treat them differently:

- Ignoring Influencer 2 because it's not worth investing in them to get their interest up.

- Keeping Organisation 8 informed with minimum effort because of their high interest but low influence. Organisation 8 could be a good example of you proving your expert knowledge and strategy. Because of the interest levels, the client may see them as important. But because of their influence levels, you can advise that there are more important targets.

(4) You'd probably ignore Influencer 7 completely.

There are many benefits of prioritising target organisations and individuals this way, including:

• It explains to the client why you are focusing on certain organisations or individuals.

• It protects you against the user buyer's desire to see a big list on the basis that more must be better, regardless of whether the people concerned have any influence/power over the client's audiences.

• It enables you and your people to be more in control of how much effort you have to put in to reach the most important audiences, which can significantly reduce overservicing and, therefore, make your work more profitable.

You could create other tools like this one to identify the reach of the outlet in terms of how much reach they have with the client's target audiences. Alternatively, you could add reach to the tool above to make the prioritisation of outlets even clearer.

This particular example shows how a tool of this kind not only puts you in control of what is done but also helps clients understand why other things will **not** be done. It will prompt a discussion that makes your client focus on their business priorities and enables you to talk about the value that will be delivered by doing what you plan to do.

In-Depth Research

Many agencies say they carry out in-depth research. But what kind of research? And why is the insight or data that is surfaced so important to delivering the client's outcome? How you define this could be one of your differentiators.

By connecting to the prioritisation tools above, you could show that your research always focuses on:

• Interest in the topic

• Influence over target audiences

• Reach into target audiences

You could also explain to the client why staying abreast of things is one of the many reasons why you deliver more value to clients than other agencies. This would help you to command a premium for your work, to reward you for the expert knowledge that your people possess, and that they have to work so hard to gather and keep current.

TOOLS TO APPEAL TO THE CLIENTS' NEED FOR CERTAINTY AND ROI

If you believe that focusing on a client's most important outcomes is central to your ability to charge according to the value you deliver, it makes sense to build prioritisation into everything you do.

Prioritising Action to Focus on the Outcomes the Client Values Most – And Limit Scope Creep

In the Introduction we talked about the cost of overservicing. This is often caused by accepting an ill-defined brief that fails to identify the client's business priorities. And without those priorities being established, it's hard to protect against scope creep, or establish the value that you will deliver.

Chart 8 shows how you can use a client's priority outcomes to decide where you will focus most effort. It's a simple spider graph. But as the BCG example proves, simple to understand charts can be very powerful.

Chart 8 does the following:

(1) It lists the client's outcomes in priority order. You could add specific labels, for example Outcome #1 – Moving to #2 in the market.

(2) It captures where the client is positioned today in relation to each outcome.

   • You could agree this position in a workshop with the client based on their current performance against the criteria they use to measure the success of the outcome.

(3) It captures where the client would like to be by the end of the year (or any chosen period).

Where To Focus Effort

────Current position   ────Desired position at end of year

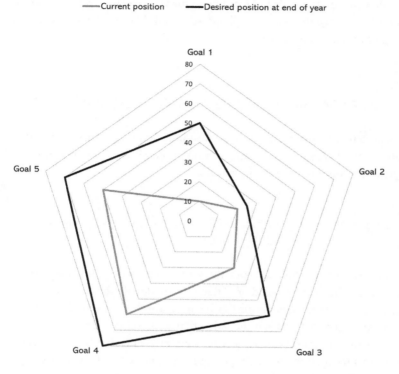

©Crispin Manners

Source: Author's own work.

Chart 8. Prioritising Where to Focus Effort.

- You could agree this position in a workshop with the client based on how they will measure the success of the outcome. This helps to establish the measurement criteria you need to know to be able to prove the value that you deliver.

Once the positions are fixed on the spider graph, you could use the gaps between the current and desired position to help explain why you will follow a specific strategy to ensure your effort is focused on delivering the best ROI for the client.

For example, you could say that it makes sense to focus most of your effort on Outcomes #1 and #3.

Outcome #1 is the most important to the business and has the biggest gap to close. It's obvious that if you can show how you contribute to closing this gap – you won't be the only contributor – your contribution will be seen as very valuable, and you can price accordingly.

It also enables you to highlight HOW your contribution will be made, so that it is easier to report on your success as you pass each milestone on the journey to the destination. You can capture this in an explicit statement of work.

While Outcome #2 is the second most valuable to the business, the gap to fill is quite small. Consequently, you could show how you would dedicate a modest amount of effort to close that gap by carrying out very specific actions. Alternatively, you could establish the value to the client of going further than the desired position and show how you would make that possible. You can capture this in an explicit statement of work.

Outcome #3 has a much bigger gap to fill than Outcome #2. You could, therefore, agree that, like Outcome #1, you will focus effort to close the gap. You can capture how you will do that in an explicit statement of work.

Once you develop a prioritisation tool of this type, you can use it to surface those priorities on a regular basis. For example, you could explain to clients that you will expect to confirm their business priorities on a quarterly basis to ensure that your strategy is always focused on delivering the outcomes that deliver the best ROI possible.

Visual tools that enable you to take your clients on the 'journey' of your thinking will gain more commitment from your client to your strategy and plan. By involving them in this way, you will trigger Robert Cialdini's law of Commitment and Consistency,[1] which means decisions that your client goes on to make are most likely to be consistent with the commitment you secured with your tool.

The Benefits of a Differentiated Approach

There are many benefits to having a differentiated approach, with the tools to support it. These include:

- Clients experience your difference each time you engage with them.

- Your people have tools that enable them to have more control over the work that is done for a client, because the client understands why it is being done that way.

- Clients recognise they have an agency rather than individual consultant experience, and are, therefore, more loyal to the agency if an individual leaves the agency.

- Your agency is clearly different at the point of sale – thus making it easier for clients to choose you from other agencies that are vanilla.

- It's easier for you to build confidence and belief in your approach, because it's easier for clients to understand why your approach is capable of delivering outcomes.

- It's easier to present your people as EXPERTS and, therefore, attract clients who need expert advice and services.

- The agency has branded intellectual property (IP) which increases the value of the agency should it ever be sold.

By using visual tools of this type, you won't have to move too far from what you already do every day to change from mis-selling time to selling value.

CHECKLIST

(1) Have you identified the key steps in your methodology, and how each step can be supported by specific visual tools?

(2) Have you checked that the tools you create help you to avoid describing your approach in the language other agencies use?

(3) Have you identified tools that enable you to involve your clients at key stages in the development of your strategy so that they become committed to your strategy?

(4) Do your tools satisfy the clients' need for prioritisation, and make everything you do focus on delivering client outcomes in the most effective way – thus reducing or eliminating overservicing?

6

HOW TO CREATE PREMIUM PRICED SERVICES THAT BREAK THE TIME TO PRICE EQUATION

One thing that never ceases to surprise me, when I work with an agency for the first time, is how little they value what they deliver for clients. And how little they use this business value to attract new clients. The main reason seems to be that they don't focus on the outcome to be delivered but the actions that will achieve the outcome. Nor do they highlight the value of the outputs and outcomes achieved. As a result, both the client and the agency take the value of what the agency achieves for granted.

The net result of behaving in this way is that it is very hard to command a premium price for work that is undertaken.

To put this in perspective, let's take as an example an agency that specialises in the toy sector. When I worked with them to surface the value they deliver, I learned that 75% of the toys that featured on the TV show that has the most influence over Christmas toy sales came from their clients! This is despite the fact that the producer of the show is bombarded by countless other agencies and brands, for hundreds if not thousands of toys. Furthermore, 100% of the toys that featured in the national newspaper, which has the most influential Christmas toy roundup, were from this agency's clients. And yet, until that point, they had not highlighted these achievements in their marketing to accentuate their expert capability. Nor had they accentuated the impact those achievements had on their clients' sales. The impact of those outputs in the media helped one client achieve the No. 6 position in NPD's Top 10 best-selling toys for Christmas, despite the fact that the product wasn't even launched, or available for sale, until three months before Christmas.

I'm sure you will agree that this is stellar work. And that work of this impact should command a premium that goes well beyond the time that was expended. While the outputs are undoubtedly impressive, it's how they contribute to the outcome of exceptional sales performance at Christmas that the client will value most.

Until you recognise the value of your work, you won't be able to charge a price that is commensurate with the value you deliver.

BREAKING THE TIME TO PRICE EQUATION

If, today, you price according to time, shifting to value-based pricing may seem like a very big leap. But many agencies that price according to time already have services that break the time to price equation.

An obvious example is media training.

Media training promotes a clear cause and effect in advance. It takes someone (the trainee) who doesn't know how to speak to the media effectively and turns them into someone who does. There is a clear value exchange where the trainee pays the trainer to take advantage of their **expert capability**. The output of this expertise – learning a new skill – is worth a premium. The outcome of being able to speak to the media effectively – such as protecting the brand from brand damage – is worth even more.

If we price media training according to the time it takes, the calculation may go something like this: Four hours of a PR director at £200 an hour equals a total price of $4 \times £200 = £800$.

If we price to achieve a premium for the value of the output and outcome, we might charge a competitive price of £400 per trainee. If you train four people in the same session, the price is $4 \times £400 = £1,600$. In other words, the session delivers an £800 premium over the time-based calculation. That's a 100% uplift over the time price. You could charge £1600 to train one person if you connect what is being taught to a business priority. Put another way the session delivers £400 per hour not the usual £200 an hour. If you develop your reputation for being the best in the business, you can probably charge more than the 'competitive' rate because you are seen as the greatest expert.

Imagine if you doubled your current rate for every hour you work!

Some people reading this will most likely be saying that this is impossible. But why? It's not impossible, you are just choosing not to make it possible.

BEING AN EXPERT IS THE FOUNDATION FOR COMMANDING A PREMIUM PRICE

The media training example works because the trainer is an expert. The Global VP for Brand Marketing of a huge technology company recently said to me that the best advice she has received in her career is: *'You need to seek out people who know more than you. Find the experts and work with them. You must run towards expertise, not away from it'.*

LOOKING LIKE AN EXPERT

So presenting you and your people as experts is essential to commanding a premium.

Again, many readers will most likely say that the senior people may qualify as experts, but the more junior team do not. This all depends on how you present your people to the market – the labels you give them. A lot of agencies accentuate lack of experience with the job titles they use, like junior account executive. They choose job titles to signal career progression rather than increasing expertise, for example: account executive, account manager, account director. The expertise associated with these job titles is at best implicit. The trick is to make it explicit.

The definition of an expert is: *A person who is very knowledgeable about, or skilful in, a particular area.* In other words, being an expert covers knowledge or skills, or both. People you may assign a junior job title to today might have a lot of knowledge or skill in a particular subject like social media, or a certain platform on social media, like TikTok. If this is the case, it makes sense to present them as your TikTok expert, not just an account manager.

Make sure the labels you apply to your people accentuate, rather than hide their expert capability.

ACTING LIKE AN EXPERT

If being an expert embraces knowledge and skills, then you can reinforce your expert status – and that of your team – by accentuating what they know, or their skills.

From a skills perspective, you can show how your team uses particular tools to deliver a particular output or outcome. Consultants at BCG are seen as experts because they use the BCG Matrix to a client's advantage. So, if you have tools that increase the certainty of outputs or outcomes of value being delivered, that are unique to your agency, the people that use them can be presented as experts. Chapter 5 gave some examples of how to create simple tools that reinforce your expert approach. It makes sense to create these tools to bring the way you deliver value to life, and to give your people the platform to behave like experts.

From a knowledge perspective, it makes sense for your TikTok expert to demonstrate their expert status by sharing knowledge about TikTok, and how that knowledge helped a client succeed, on a regular basis.

Because many agencies look at these things from a hierarchical perspective, their agency only presents a small number of senior people as experts, thus limiting the expert authority of the agency. It says to clients that if they choose this agency, they will have a few smart people, and a lot of others who are just implementors. This inevitably leads to clients insisting they have access to the most senior people, when this is neither necessary nor desirable for either party. Of course, some of your team won't yet have the knowledge or skills to be credible as experts, all the more reason to find ways to bring the full range of knowledge and skill that your team possesses to the surface. And to eliminate time drains so you can develop experts more quickly.

To reinforce your expert status – and that of your team – make sure you bring the full range of knowledge and skill, that you and your team possesses, to the surface.

DON'T MISS THE OPPORTUNITY TO COMMAND A PREMIUM PRICE BY HIDING VALUABLE CONTRIBUTIONS IN A 'RETAINER' APPROACH

Abraham Lincoln is attributed with the saying: *'If I only had an hour to chop down a tree, I would spend the first 45 minutes sharpening my axe'.*

If we apply this to the agency world, it means that smart agencies put a lot of thinking up front before they start work. In essence, they think about the smartest way to deliver the outputs or outcomes the client is seeking.

However, when I help agency leaders surface the HOW of their agency, it often becomes clear that the smart thinking is given away free as part of the pitch process, or as part of the retainer. In other words, the agency uses all its expert knowledge and skill to create a strategy, or ideas for a campaign, and neither demonstrates their expert capability by involving the client in the creation of the strategy, or ideas, nor charges them for the ability to *'chop the tree down faster because the axe is razor sharp'.*

If you do this, you will miss the opportunity to accentuate your expert status and be rewarded for the value this provides the client.

So my advice is to identify where on the journey, from a brief to an output or outcome a client values, you contribute the most value. Identify where you have the expert knowledge, skill or process that makes their desired outcome more certain.

There are some obvious candidates for a premium priced service. Many agencies will already deliver services of this type, which proves it can be done.

- **Helping the client prioritise where they invest their communications effort.**
  Most clients know there are hundreds of things they could do. What they want to know is which will deliver a more certain ROI. If, like BCG, you help clients prioritise, you can break the time to price equation. For example, you could develop a prioritisation workshop. It might last four hours and take two of your people. A normal senior hour rate (say £250 an hour) would be priced at £2,000. But because you are meeting an important need for certainty, you could charge more, maybe £5,000, or perhaps £10,000. A lot will depend on the size and type of client.

- **Developing a communications strategy.**
  At the very least, you could create a price for the strategy based on the time it's taken the team to develop it. But you don't need to present the price as related to time – just the price for 'sharpening the axe'. This is already a much more valuable outcome for you than 'including it in the pitch or retainer'. But if you had a 'sharpening the axe' service that involved the client in the development of the strategy – following the key elements of your HOW – then, not only would you reinforce their belief and confidence in your expert knowledge and skills, but you would also be able to charge a value-based price.

- **Developing messages that trigger the right action.**
  Like the strategy development above, you can develop messages remotely, or you can have a service that involves the client in the development of messages. It's your choice.
  The benefit of having a workshop that involves the client is that you will trigger the psychology of involvement, and Robert Cialdini's Law of Commitment and Consistency.[1] By being involved in the creation of the strategy or the messages, the client will be committed to using them and, as a result, the decisions they make thereafter will tend to be consistent with that commitment – putting your agency in a powerful position.

- **Developing campaign ideas.** Like the message development above, you can develop campaign ideas remotely, or you can have a service that involves the client in the development of campaigns. If you involve the client in an ideation workshop, it will deliver several benefits. It will enable the client to experience your creative genius, and creative process, and therefore not take idea creation for granted. It will expose them to a range of options that they may not have seen if you developed ideas remotely – thus priming them for future campaigns. It will train them to expect to pay for ideas, and therefore value ideas more than they would if they were delivered free.

  If you develop ideas in a pitch, does that mean you miss out on being able to charge for the ideas if selected? It all depends on how you set expectations with the client ahead of the pitch, and whether ideation is part of your HOW. In my experience, clients often choose an agency because they liked their ideas, only for those ideas not to be implemented. This is because the ideas showed the client how the agency thought about them, their challenges and the outcome they wanted delivered. So my advice is to explain to clients that you will create ideas for the proposal/pitch, but when selected will expect to run an ideation workshop – with a clear price – to get agreement on the ideas that will be pursued.

Some readers might be anxious that charging for prioritisation, strategy, messages and ideas might mean that there isn't enough left in a budget to deliver the campaigns. This may be true. It's because we have trained clients to expect to get them 'free'. An architect doesn't say we'll give you the design free and charge you for the technical drawings!

So don't be constrained by the quoted budget, be liberated by the value of the outcome the client wants to achieve.

If you involve clients in the process of 'sharpening the axe', they will have more belief in your ability to deliver the outputs and outcomes they want. If you've shown them how this delivers an effective return on investment, they will find the money needed to achieve it. If they can't then they may not be an ideal client for you!

USE YOUR PREMIUM SERVICES TO OPEN DOORS WITH TARGET CLIENTS

The benefit of developing and marketing expert, premium priced services of the type above, is that you can use them to open doors with clients on your target list AND develop a healthy revenue and profit stream that breaks the time to price equation.

Doing this can significantly reduce your cost of sales. It's highly likely that if a client has worked with you to develop a strategy or campaign, they will want to work with you to deliver what has been created together.

If you create premium priced services that involve the client, you will build belief and confidence in your expert capability to deliver the outputs and outcomes they most want to achieve.

CHECKLIST

(1) Do you bring the valuable outputs and outcomes you achieve to the surface?

(2) Do you quantify the value of the outputs and outcomes in a way that is meaningful to the client?

(3) Do you accentuate the expert knowledge and skills of all your people in a way that reinforces your HOW?

(4) Do you enable you and your people to behave like experts?

(5) Have you developed the tools that reinforce their expertise?

(6) Have you separated your 'sharpening the axe' services from the amorphous mire of a retainer?

(7) Do you use your premium priced, expert services to build confidence and belief in all your services?

(8) Do you use your premium priced expert services to open doors with the clients you most want to work with?

(9) Do you use your premium priced expert services to build a healthy revenue and profit stream that breaks the time to price equation?

7

HOW TO SET A VALUE-BASED PRICE

As the Introduction said, agencies like time-based pricing because creating a time-based price is straightforward. You know how many people you have. You know how many billable hours they have. You know your other costs. And you know how much profit you'd like to make. Put all that together and you can create a price per hour for each role in your business.

Chapter One highlighted the many flaws of pricing using time. Chapter Six identified how straightforward it is to break the time-to-price equation. This chapter covers how to set a value-based price.

Unfortunately, the equation isn't as simple as the time-based approach. But there are many rewards for getting it right, including:

- Significantly more profit – and, therefore, wealth for you and everyone in your agency.

- Less pressure on time – and, therefore, better work–life balance.

- More enjoyable work – and, therefore, a happier and more productive team.

Before we look at calculating a value-based price, remember, you have a choice for when you use value-based pricing. It doesn't have to be an all or nothing pricing approach.

But the more you can take a progressive approach to secure your future, by eliminating waste from the way you operate, and presenting and pricing your services according to how they deliver greater certainty of value to clients, the more likely you are to succeed.

THE COMPONENTS OF THE VALUE PRICING EQUATION

There are some clear components in the calculation, see below.

Value of client's business objective	Cost of alternative approaches	Value of your contribution to achieving objective	Perception of your expert status

Calculating the Value of Achieving a Client's Business Objective – Or the Cost of Not Achieving It

As the heading suggests, there are usually two areas of value related to a client's business objective that you can calculate in advance – the value of success and the cost of failure.

Chapter Two looks at some of the questions you can ask a client to establish this value in advance. We will use the example below to explore this further.

Calculating the Cost of Alternative Approaches

Clients will often have alternative options for achieving their objective. It makes sense to understand the price of the other options. You can calculate that by asking the client the right questions or by calculating it logically behind the scenes.

Calculating the Value of Your Contribution to Achieving a Client's Business Objective

As Chapter Two says, you don't have to be the only contributor to achieving an objective for your contribution to be valuable. You don't have to impact every step on a journey. But you need to be able to show where you can make a difference.

By identifying where you make a valuable contribution, you have created a way to be connected with the value of the objective.

Calculating the Value of the Perception of Your Expert Status

It's a truism in any market that the people who are seen as the most effective command the highest prices. We used the football (soccer) analogy earlier about goal scorers, but the same applies to chefs, hairdressers, lawyers, tax accountants etc.

The more you build the perception of your expert knowledge and skills, the higher the premium you can add to what might be seen as a market price. A big part of this component of value pricing comes down to confidence – the confidence of you, your team and the client in your ability to deliver outcomes. That's why you need to focus on building belief and confidence through the way you present your WHY, your HOW and the proof that you deliver outcomes of value.

A Value Pricing Example

Imagine that a private equity backed company that delivers in-home optometry services asks you to deliver a project to help them recruit optometrists. The brief is a simple one – to raise awareness and understanding of the company to help attract optometrists. This is a typical user buyer brief. Your first job is to convert this into an economic buyer brief to understand the difference you will make to the business.

A typical time-based response to this brief would be to get the right messages used by the right influencers. As a simple activity, where you provided your ideas/strategy free of charge, let's imagine that the estimated total number of hours multiplied by the hourly rates produced a fee of £10,000.

Now let's build a price by working through the components of a value-based price.

(1) **Calculating the value of achieving a client's business objective – or the cost of not achieving it**
    The client needs to hire 80 optometrists to hit its growth targets and release further investor support for future growth. It needs to hire the optometrists as soon as possible; otherwise revenue will not be generated. So what do you need to know?

    - What is the salary of each optometrist?
      – Answer: £75,000.

    - How much revenue can an optometrist support each month?
      – Answer: 3x salary divided by 12 = £18,750 per month.

- By when does each optometrist need to be active for the company to hit revenue targets?
  - Answer: 15 by end of Q1, another 40 by end of Q2 and another 25 by end of Q3.

- Why is the client asking you to help them?
  - Answer: Because they aren't recruiting enough people fast enough.

- What other methods are being used?
  - Answer: Recruitment agencies and employee referral incentive.

- Why aren't these other methods working?
  - Answer: The applicants they get don't convert to an offer. Half of the people that join leave before the end of their trial period.

  - You can ask further questions about the current number of applicants a month and the conversion:
    - from application to interview.

    - from interview to job offer.

    - from job offer of acceptance.

    - from successful applicant to successful completion of the trial.

There are other questions you can ask, but the answers above have already given you valuable information on which to base a value-based price. You now know:

- The salary.

- The revenue generated per person per month.

- The speed at which optometrists need to arrive.

- The failure points in the process.

- The current conversion rates at each step on the journey from applicant interest to hired optometrists and optometrists that stay.

From this information, you can calculate the value added if recruits arrive earlier than expected – each month delivering an additional £18,750 for each recruit. You can also calculate the cost of recruits arriving late – £18,750 for each recruit per month.

You also know that achieving the revenue target is pivotal to future success. **Put another way, the help they want has real strategic importance – it's really to help them stay on the growth path by achieving their revenue target, not just hire people.**

Some readers may already be saying: '*This is too complicated; we'd never ask questions like that or get the answers if we did.*' It is more complicated than pricing time, but stick with the example to see where it goes.

(2) **Calculating the cost of alternative approaches**
We know that the client has been using (and may continue to use) recruitment agents and employee incentives.

You know (or can deduce) that the client pays 25% of the salary for each recruit that comes through a recruitment company. You know they pay employees £750 for each successful referral. So the cost of using agents is as follows:

- Each recruit costs: £75,000 × 25% = £18,750.

- 80 recruits cost: 80 × £18,750 = £1.5 million.

If we stop here, we already know that the client is prepared to pay £1.5 million to recruit 80 people.

So why charge only £10,000 to help them? The recruitment company doesn't estimate the time it will take to provide a price, so why should you? They also don't bring successful recruits, just opportunities to interview – and this currently isn't working!

(3) **Calculating the value of your contribution to achieving a client's business objective**
Based on what we know, where on the journey can you make a valuable contribution? There are a number of areas:

- You can increase the number of applicants by raising awareness.

- You can educate and excite potential applicants, so they arrive for an interview in the right frame of mind. This could include setting expectations about the company, the purpose of the role (in this case ensuring that the vision of people who lack the mobility to get to an optician does not suffer), the content of the role, the rewards.

- You can remove or reduce any anxieties about the job security of joining a PE-backed company, so more people apply.

As you can see above, you have clearly identified for the client where (which steps on the journey) you can make a valuable contribution. And, by monitoring the data at each step, you can prove how your work has enhanced the performance of the process and, therefore, reduced the cost.

Operating in this way shows the client the cause and effect of using you, and reinforces why a value-based price is deserved.

And you can track when the recruits arrive to demonstrate the value delivered of them arriving early.

You can also create upselling opportunities. They invited you to help them hire people, but you've identified that retention through the trial isn't good. So you could propose helping them improve the onboarding process with the right communications, so people receive an employee experience that gives them reasons to stay.

(4) **Calculating the value of the perception of your expert status**
Imagine if you operate in this way all the time. And imagine if you publish the proof of the value you deliver in terms that are compelling to economic buyers, not just user buyers. Imagine you have an explicit methodology that increases the certainty of delivering the outcome and that you use that method to show, in advance, where and how you will deliver value. The net result of all of those things will be the opportunity to charge a premium over lesser agencies.

What could you charge?
So what could/should you charge in this example?

- If you could bring 80 successful recruits, the opportunity is £1.5 million.

  - But the client is unlikely to dispense with recruitment companies and switch everything to you.

- So your price could relate to the fact that you:

  - Will increase the quality of applicants, and the performance of the process at the steps where you identified the strongest contribution.

- Will bring some applicants straight to the client – thus avoiding the cost of a recruitment agency.

- Improve the conversion from applicant to offer – thus:

  • Saving a lot of client time.

  • Bringing through recruits faster – and, therefore, enhanced revenue performance.

• It's at this point you break with the traditional approach of showing the client how much time it will take you to do something. Instead, you show them the financial value of the various ways you will deliver value. For example:

  - For each recruit that avoids the agency route, you will save the client £18,750. Just bringing one recruit direct delivers more value than the original £10,000 price.

  - For each recruit that arrives a month early, you add £18,750 to the revenue.

  - Just doing the two things above for one recruit for one month is £37,500. Imagine you did that for three out of the 80 recruits, then it's worth £112,500 to the client.

• While you can't guarantee three recruits, or them arriving early, you can show the client enough certainty of your positive impact for them to take a calculated risk. After all, they know other routes aren't delivering what they need.

MAKE IT EASY FOR THE CLIENT TO ACCEPT YOUR PRICE BY SHOWING HOW YOUR CONTRIBUTION DELIVERS MORE VALUE THAN THE ALTERNATIVE OPTIONS

So what should the price be? Your goal here is to make it easy for the client to accept your price by showing how your contribution delivers more value than the alternative options. For example, just bringing one recruit direct is worth £18,750, so the price should be at least that. But you can show many other ways you can add value, such as the extra revenue from optometrists arriving early. Then it's down to how confident you are that your approach will improve the performance of the process. The more confident you are, and the more your approach increases the certainty of impact, the more you can increase the price. So should it be £18,750 or £50,000 or even £112,500, that's your choice.

But by taking a value-based approach, you have moved the time-based price up from £10,000 to something significantly higher, thus delivering a significantly better return for the time invested. You have also shown the client where you will add value, and what data needs to be captured and shared to prove that value. We will look at data, and how to visualise the impact of your work, in future chapters.

Of course, you could choose to de-risk the decision for a client even further. You could choose to provide an option for an initial project to prove how you will improve their process. The expectation would be that when you show the improvement – more applicants arriving direct, better conversions etc. – they would hire you to do the same again, whilst also defocusing on recruitment agencies now they know they don't need them as much. This would enable you to charge a higher fee the second time round.

This example above shows the huge value that is often left on the table by an agency by pricing according to time. By linking what you do to contributing to delivering a business outcome that an economic buyer cares about, you will create the opportunity to price according to the value you deliver.

CHECKLIST

(1) Have you asked the questions that enable you to calculate the value of a client's business objective?

(2) Have you identified the strategic importance of achieving that objective?

(3) Have you identified the alternative approaches being used, and the cost of alternative approaches?

(4) Have you identified the performance of existing approaches, and captured the data associated with this performance?

(5) Have you identified the steps on the journey to the objective/outcome where you can provide the most value?

(6) Have you made explicit to the client your contribution, and HOW you will deliver it?

(7) Have you built a strong perception of your expert knowledge, skills and methodology to be able to command a premium?

(8) Have you quantified the value of achieving parts of the objective, to create the foundation for your price?

(9) Have you made it easy to accept your price, by showing how your contribution delivers more value than the alternative options?

8

THE IMPORTANCE OF ACCESS TO CLIENT DATA THAT IDENTIFIES AND PROVES THE VALUE YOU DELIVER

This chapter covers the importance of having access to a client's data to underpin a value-based price and prove the value delivered to a client.

The barriers about data that are often mentioned to me include:

- The client doesn't or won't share data with us.

- I don't know what data to ask for.

- We aren't the only contributor to outcomes achieved.

Let's use a real-life scenario to identify the data that is needed and how to persuade the client to provide access to it.

During a training session I was delivering on how to control overservicing, I got to the point in the session when I said that agencies need to ask clients to share data. There were two people on the training from an in-house PR department of an online betting company. The PR Manager challenged me and said: *Why would I share data with my agency? All I ask them to do is secure links in online coverage that enable online betters to visit our website. They don't need any data; they just need to hit the link target I set them.*

So, I asked the in-house PR manager why she didn't provide data to the agency on the performance of each of these links. She said that her agency had never asked for access to any data but asked me why that was necessary as she measured the agency performance on the number of links secured.

So, I asked her if all betters were equal. She said that they were not, and that they were most interested in attracting what she called a highly engaged better (HEB) – someone who spent more money.

At this point I'm sure you are way ahead of me. It's obvious that, if the agency had access to the data on the performance of the various links they secured, they would be able to identify which sites and messages delivered HEBs most effectively. By having access to this data, they could adapt and evolve what they did to ensure that they improved the return on investment for the client by bringing through more HEBs – thus making their contribution much more valuable.

Unsurprisingly, the PR manager said that made a lot of sense, and also said that she would set up a meeting with her agency to refine the brief and agree what data to share.

This is a good example of an agency focusing on WHAT they do not WHY they do it. If they wanted to really prove their value, they would have looked beyond the link to what the link delivered to the business.

It's also a good example of a communications brief developed by a user buyer. If the economic buyer had written the brief, it would probably have said something like:

- Help us hit our revenue targets by attracting more HEBs.

- Increase our profit and effectiveness by increasing the proportion of HEBs in our customer base.

To enable you to identify the value you will deliver, and be able to price for that valuable contribution, you should not accept a WHAT level brief. You must convert it into a WHY level brief.

If you don't surface the business value of what the client is trying to achieve, it will be impossible to prove the value of what you deliver.

WHAT DATA SHOULD THE AGENCY HAVE ASKED FOR?

Before you get into the data, it's important to ask some other questions of yourselves, and the client, to identify the journey that the work represents. Questions that identify the WHY behind the work and where and HOW you can contribute the most value.

(1) What is the destination the client wants to reach – expressed in terms of business objectives?
   a. In this example, now we know about the HEBs, we know there is a revenue objective to be surfaced. But is this to grow the business or to recover from a recent loss of betters to competitors?

(2) Where are we starting from? What is the current performance?

  a. As 1a shows, we could be starting from a position of strength or weakness. In both cases your contribution could be valuable.

(3) What is the financial value of closing the gap – reaching the destination?

  a. This crystallises the value against which your contribution will be assessed. It's a lot easier to command a premium price if you help generate £10 million than if you deliver 100 links.

(4) What is the strategic value of reaching the destination?

  a. As 1a and 1b show, there will be a more important goal than just the revenue.

(5) At which steps on the journey can we contribute most?

  a. By asking questions about current performance, you may be able to identify other places on the journey where you can contribute – see below.

Based on this example, it would make sense for the agency to ask the questions below to be able to assess the value of their contribution:

(1) The number/proportion of betters that are HEBs today.

(2) The target number/proportion at the end of the year.

(3) The average financial value of a HEB.

(4) Other categories of better that exist, in the order of value to the client.

(5) The proportion of people who arrive via a link that go on to bet.

(6) The proportion of those that bet more than once.

SPECIFIC DATA TO REQUEST

(1) The type of better that arrives via each link.

  a. This will enable you to identify which outlets and messages bring through different categories – thus enabling you to segment outlets and messages for future targeting.

(2) The behaviour of the better on arrival.

    a. This will enable you to assess which messages not only attract betters but trigger the right action from betters. You can't control the messaging on the website, but you could influence or even contribute to it.

WHY SHOULD A CLIENT SHARE THIS DATA?

If you explain to a client that your goal is to deliver as much value as possible from your work, it then becomes logical for you to evaluate (not just measure) what is working, and what isn't, so you can make improvements. In this case, you can't evaluate and improve without having data about the category of better and their betting behaviour.

If the client shares the data and you show how this enables improved performance of their process, you have created a powerful reason for them to keep using you, and maybe using you in other parts of their business.

You can't evaluate and improve what you do without data. By showing a client why it is in their best interests – both as a user buyer and as an organisation – you make it possible to prove your value and command a premium price that is related to the value you deliver.

As can be seen from the example above, the right data can enable you to:

- Calculate the financial and business value of your agency's contribution.

- Prove the value of your agency's contribution. And use this to build your EXPERT reputation.

- Show that your agency has a desire to evaluate what it does to improve ROI for the client.

- Sell back the value of your contribution.

- Show that there is a cause and effect in terms of the value delivered by your agency's work – thus showing how you effectively guarantee a ROI.

- Be more in control of what is done and by whom at your agency.

EXPANDING THE BRIEF – AND THE VALUE YOU DELIVER

As mentioned above, once you've identified the business WHY of the work, you can, if you choose to, find ways to expand the brief. In the HEB example above, your agency cannot control what happens when a HEB lands on the site. But if the data shows there is a poor conversion, you can advise on the content on the landing page, so it matches with the content of the article that contained the link. This way the article you help to create can include messages that make sure the HEB is in the right frame of mind to take the right action on arrival. By expanding your contribution to a wider sales and marketing process, and not just media relations, you will increase the perceived value of your contribution and access other lucrative budgets.

WHAT DATA SHOULD WE ASK FOR IF THE WHY IS LONGER TERM OR NOT TRANSACTIONAL?

The first thing to establish is the business WHY.

In Chapter Two we looked at longer-term goals such as achieving a licence to operate, getting approval for a drug, winning an election, getting planning permission for a new development or changing a law.

If you have been hired to help achieve a long-term WHY, it's essential for you to identify where on the journey to achieving the WHY, the destination, that your contribution is essential or very important.

Once you've identified the steps where you can contribute best, you can identify what data the client needs to share so that you can perform at your best. For the specialists that focus on the long-term outcomes above, the data they need may be obvious. For example, to help win an election, your agency might be writing speeches or preparing for a live debate. Having access to data on the response to the speech or debate is obviously vital to what you do next.

So, in many respects PR experts automatically identify data requirements to prove their value for non-transactional work. Why is that? After all, it should be easier to identify data for work related to clear transactions.

I believe the answer lies in surfacing the WHY. In the long-term examples above, there is a clear WHY – winning an election for example. In the online betting example, the brief didn't include the business WHY and the agency didn't surface it. That's because many agencies see media relations as an end in itself – rather than a contributor to achieving a outcome or business WHY.

Don't see WHAT you do as an end in itself. Always surface the WHY behind the WHAT if you want to be rewarded for the value you deliver.

WHAT DATA SHOULD WE ASK FOR WHEN WE HAVE A RETAINER?

In Chapter Two we highlighted the weakness of the traditional 'retainer' model. It demonstrates that an agency is only thinking about WHAT they do and not WHY they are doing it.

Before you can identify the data you need to evaluate the value of your contribution, you need to identify the WHY behind why the client is contracting to work with you over a long period. Just like the online betting example, if the client says the retainer is to raise awareness, or something relatively amorphous like that, you need to ask the *why does that matter* question until you surface the business WHY. This is the case whether it is at the start of a retainer relationship or the beginning of your 10th year with the client.

It's possible that the retainer – the long-term contract – might address multiple business outcomes. In this case, you need to identify where you will contribute on the journey to each destination. Once that is established, the data you need will become much more obvious.

By adopting this approach, the client will be able to identify the value you deliver rather than just seeing you as a cost on a budget line.

CHECKLIST

(1) Have you surfaced the WHY behind the WHAT – i.e. converted a WHAT brief into a WHY brief?

(2) Have you quantified the financial value of reaching the destination – achieving the WHY?

(3) Have you quantified the strategic value of reaching the destination – achieving the WHY?

(4) Have you identified the steps on the journey where you contribute?

(5) Have you quantified the starting point, and therefore the gap, and the financial value of filling the gap, to the destination?

(6) Have you identified how the client measures success, and the data they use to do that?

(7) Have you explained the benefit to the individual (the user buyer) and the organisation (the economic buyer) of sharing this data with you?

(8) Have you used the data that is captured to crystallise and sell back the value that you deliver?

9

HOW YOUR TEAM CAN GET THE USER BUYER TO EMBRACE A VALUE-BASED APPROACH

Switching to selling value, rather than time, not only represents a significant behaviour shift for an agency but also for user buyers. So, this chapter will show how to get the team to sell value in a way that keeps a user buyer satisfied and supportive. Done correctly, selling value will enable you to set client expectations in a way that puts you more in control of what your team does and how they do it.

The challenge to be overcome is that user buyers use different language to economic buyers, have different priorities and expect to measure activity in a different way to economic buyers.

PRIORITISATION IS THE KEY TO SWITCHING FROM TIME TO VALUE

One of the objectives of making the switch from selling time to selling value is to break the time to revenue equation. If you achieve this, you will be able to increase revenues without adding people, and you will be able to remove many of the reasons for overservicing.

The key to making the shift successfully is to embrace and embed the power of prioritisation.

Throughout the book, I have made the point that everything starts with surfacing the WHY behind the WHAT – the business outcomes the client is paying the money to help achieve. But to keep user buyers supportive, you will need to help them understand why the focus on the WHY behind the WHAT is good for them. This won't come naturally because many user buyers have been trained by agencies to expect a WHAT level focus.

However, as the online betting example showed, user buyers will embrace a new approach if they can see how it helps them do their job.

So, I recommend that you follow this approach to getting user buyers satisfied and supportive:

(1) Establish the client's business objectives at the outset and prioritise them with the client. Translate a WHAT level brief into a WHY level brief.

(2) Connect clear communications objectives to each business objective and prioritise them.

    a. This will be important because it brings what you are doing back into their domain, which will make them more comfortable.

    b. You can involve the client in a prioritisation workshop, so they come on the journey with you and are committed to the priority order identified.

(3) Change what is 'counted' by user buyers, so they understand their requests for more activity results in less rather than more value.

    a. You can capture the priorities in visual tools like those shown in Chapter Five. This will be important because user buyers like to count things. They see more as more. In other words, they measure increased value by the increase in the number of outputs, e.g. an increase in the number of titles where coverage is secured, regardless of whether those outputs have made a difference to achieving the client's business objectives. This leads to overservicing and all the pain that goes with it.

    b. This will show the user buyer how they can satisfy the economic buyer by focusing on fewer but more valuable activities and audiences. This means you and your team can avoid pointless activity.

(4) Capture the starting position for the client in an infographic that can be used thereafter to show the difference the agency has made – see Chart 9.

(5) Capture the destination for the client in an infographic that quantifies the value that reaching the destination will deliver – see Chart 10.

(6) Agree the data to quantify what is being delivered for each of the priorities.

The **WHY** of the work:

Increasing the number and proportion of Highly Engaged Betters - HEBs

# of HEBs
33,800

TOTAL HEB REVENUE

£

£319.82m

HEB Proportion
22%

new HEBs
6,200

Average HEB spend
£9,462 pa

Areas that the agency will impact most

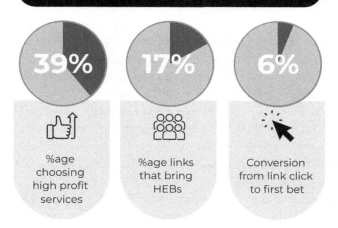

39%

%age choosing high profit services

17%

%age links that bring HEBs

6%

Conversion from link click to first bet

©Crispin Manners

Source: Author's original work.

Chart 9. The WHY of the Work-Starting Position.

(7) Use priorities, the picture of the destination, and data to stop scope creep and keep the user buyer focused on business priorities.

(8) Provide them with an economic buyer-friendly report to share with senior stakeholders in the organisation, as a companion to the user buyer report they will dictate you need to provide. This report will show the value delivered to the organisation in a high-impact, visual and shareable format.

   a. You can explain to the user buyer that this is your investment in your relationship with them. You can explain that this is to make them look good (and your agency) by making EXPLICIT your joint contribution to achieving the organisation's business objectives.

   b. This process of reinforcing the user buyer's position is essential to a stress-free day-to-day relationship.

(9) Revisit priorities on a quarterly basis to ensure that all work is focused on delivering the most valued and valuable outcomes.

Let's look at some of these actions in more detail.

CAPTURING THE STARTING POSITION IN AN INFOGRAPHIC

Clients often have very short memories and forget what their organisation, or the challenges it faced, looked like when they issued their initial brief. Client briefs rarely capture a clear picture, so it's essential that you do that if you want to be able to prove the extent, and value, of your contribution.

Many agencies will carry out a SWOT analysis which captures a lot of helpful data. But this is rarely represented in a visual picture of the challenge to be solved. So, what should you include in this 'picture'? It will very much depend on the challenge concerned. Chart 9 shows what could have been captured as the starting position for the brief provided for the online betting example in Chapter Eight.

The infographic shows the number of HEBs, the target number for new HEBs, the proportion HEBs represent of total customers, the revenue coming from HEBs, the average spend per HEB and the percentage of HEBs choosing high profit services. It shows the percentage of links bringing HEBs to the website and the conversion from a click on a link to the first bet. And it shows the steps where your agency will contribute most.

USING THE STARTING POSITION AS A REFERENCE POINT FOR PROVING VALUE

This starting picture is a very helpful tool. It is a fixed reference point for showing the user buyer (and the economic buyer) where your team will be focusing effort, and for proving the value that you contribute.

I recommend you include it in both your user and economic buyer reports.

CAPTURING THE DESTINATION IN AN INFOGRAPHIC

The starting picture pays off when it is accompanied by a picture of the destination – what the outcome to be achieved looks like.

Chart 10 captures what the client wants each of the data points in the starting picture to have become. The movements represent changes that satisfy the economic buyer – increases to the number and proportion of HEBs, increases to the average and total spend by HEBs, and the percentage choosing high profit services. There are also user buyer-oriented movements, including increases in the percentage of links that bring HEBs and the increase in the conversion from a click to a first bet.

You can explain to the user buyer:

- Your approach for making the articles that contain the links more compelling to HEBs, so that it triggers more clicks.

- How the content will be designed to encourage a first bet – and how the landing page copy should be matched to the content of the article.

- You can show the client that the things you will do are steps on the journey to the destination. This will enable you to show progress to the client on a regular basis.

USING THE STARTING AND DESTINATION PICTURE TO SHOW THE VALUE YOU WILL CREATE

Because you have both the starting and destination data points that mean something to the economic buyer, you can now calculate the value of the contribution you are being asked to make:

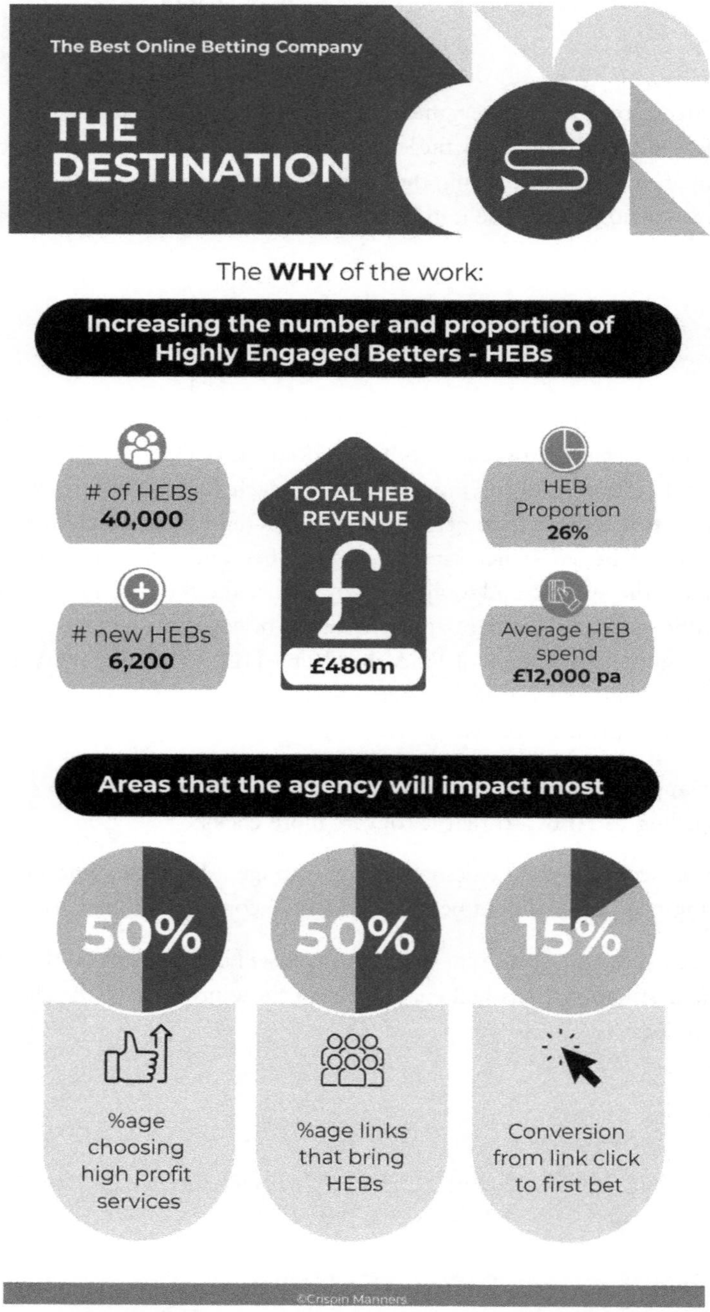

The Best Online Betting Company

THE DESTINATION

The **WHY** of the work:

Increasing the number and proportion of Highly Engaged Betters - HEBs

# of HEBs
40,000

TOTAL HEB REVENUE

£

£480m

HEB Proportion
26%

new HEBs
6,200

Average HEB spend
£12,000 pa

Areas that the agency will impact most

50%

%age choosing high profit services

50%

%age links that bring HEBs

15%

Conversion from link click to first bet

©Crispin Manners

Source: Author's original work.

Chart 10. The WHY of the Work-the Destination.

- Increase the number of HEBs by 6,200.

- Increase the proportion of HEBs by 4%.

- Increase the average spend by HEBs by 27% or £2,538 per HEB.

- Increase the total revenue from HEBs by £160m.

- Deliver revenue from the 6,200 new HEBs of £74.4m.

Once those numbers are calculated, it's clear that the contribution of your agency is much more than just securing links in coverage. Done correctly, those links will be responsible for a huge increase in revenue and profit for the client. There is certainly enough value there to command an increase in price.

But, unless you make that EXPLICIT, your client will think they are paying for PR activity, not help to generate an additional £74.4m.

USING THE DESTINATION AS A REFERENCE POINT FOR PROVING VALUE

The destination picture is a very helpful tool. It is a fixed reference point for showing both the user buyer and economic buyer why you have chosen a particular strategy. And why you need data from the client so that you can continuously evaluate the performance of each link, to drive improvement.

I recommend you include it in both your user and economic buyer reports. And then show progress towards the objective. So, each month you could show:

- How many of the 6200 HEBs have been delivered.

- How the proportion of HEBs has increased.

- The progress towards the average spend increase by HEBs.

- A calculation of the revenue delivered by new HEBs.

- Improvement in the proportion of links bringing HEBs.

- Improvement in the conversion from click to first bet.

Showing this value will not only make your agency look good, but very importantly, also make the user buyer look good too.

USING THE STARTING AND DESTINATION PICTURES TO CONTROL OVERSERVICING REQUESTS

The starting and destination 'pictures' can be used to control overservicing requests by reminding user buyers about the priorities for action, and the value to the organisation of reaching the destination. And, significantly, because the user buyer doesn't think there is a 'bank of time' to spend, they don't see the agency as an available (free) resource for non-essential work.

Of course, if you have provided the recommended Outside the Statement of Work document, the user buyer will know you are available to help – at a price.

The starting and destination pictures can also be used by the user buyer to control requests for agency support from their internal customers, by highlighting how these requests would defocus the agency's efforts from delivering high value outcomes. They could also be used to set expectations that a new budget would need to be found.

If you create a clear picture of the journey to be travelled to the client destination, you will be able to charge a value-based price, be more in control of overservicing requests and prove your value on a continuous basis.

CHECKLIST

(1) Have you established the client's business objectives at the outset, and prioritised them with the client?

(2) Have you connected clear communications objectives to each business objective, and prioritised them?

(3) Have you changed what is 'counted' by user buyers, so they understand their requests for more activity results in less rather than more value?

(4) Have you captured the priorities in visual tools like those shown in Chapter Eight?

(5) Have you captured the starting position for the client in an infographic that can be used thereafter to show the difference the agency has made?

(6) Have you captured the destination for the client in an infographic that quantifies the value that reaching the destination will deliver?

(7) Have you agreed which data needs to be provided to quantify what is being delivered for each of the priorities?

(8) Are you using the priorities, the picture of the destination and data to stop scope creep and keep the user buyer focused on business priorities?

(9) Are you providing an economic buyer-friendly report to share with senior stakeholders in the organisation, that shows the value delivered to the organisation in a high-impact, visual and sharable format?

(10) Have you explained to the user buyer that the economic buyer report is your investment to make them look good (and the agency), by making EXPLICIT their contribution to achieving the organisation's business objectives?

(11) Are you revisiting the priorities on a quarterly basis to ensure that all work is focused on delivering the most valued and valuable outcomes?

10

HOW TO CHANGE THE DAY-TO-DAY BEHAVIOUR OF ACCOUNT TEAMS TO SUPPORT THE VALUE-BASED PRICING APPROACH

If you want to make a successful transformation to selling value not time, this is where the most work will need to be done.

Getting clients to embrace the new approach will only work if your team embraces it first.

We are talking about a major change in team behaviour. They will have to unlearn some old practices and replace them with new ones.

I don't think your people will be unwilling to make the change, because the benefits to them will be significant, including:

- The work will have a clearer sense of purpose.

- Their role in achieving client outcomes will give them a greater sense of achievement.

- They will learn faster because the reasons for doing things will be clearer.

- They will not have to work so hard because overservicing levels will be reduced.

- There will be more time for their personal development.

- The enhanced profitability of the company should bring enhanced rewards for them.

So where is the best place to start?

START BY RECOGNISING THAT MINDSET MATTERS

The best way to understand how to help your people make this change is to understand how our brains work.

Fortunately, there has been some great work carried out by neuroscientists in the last couple of decades that provides helpful frameworks for what needs to be done. There is a framework called SCARF created by a neuroscientist called Dr David Rock[1] which will help you to understand why you need to do certain things to help your people make the desired changes.

SCARF is an acronym that addresses five needs our brains have for us to feel valued and happy at work. Each of the letters of SCARF will point to some essential actions by you. I've focused on the first three. The fourth, R for RELATEDNESS (how connected people feel to the organisation and their colleagues) and the fifth, F for FAIRNESS (feeling fairly treated) also need to be considered.

(1) S stands for **STATUS**, a need we have to understand our role within an organisation and how that role is valued by the organisation and the people in it.

   Moving to selling value should satisfy each individual's STATUS need because it will be clear to them that helping a client improve their business, (as in the online betting example) or improve people's health with the approval of a vaccine, is more valuable than sending out a press release or pitching a story.

   Once you understand you must satisfy this need, it will be clear that you need to change how you describe each role in the business. This will include job descriptions so that they become more outcome oriented. This doesn't mean that all the tasks people carry out will change; it means that the way you describe the purpose and importance of the role changes.

   This sense of purpose should be reinforced by the way you provide a brief to a team so that you emphasise the importance of each task they will carry out.

   STATUS can also be reinforced by creating economic buyer reports where the value the individual contributed to creating is made crystal clear.

(2) C is for **CERTAINTY** – a need we have to understand what will happen next. If something changes in your business, but the implications of this change are not explained, this will cause anxiety. So it is vital that you explain why you are changing from selling time to selling value, and what this means to everyone in the business.

It also means that you will need to give your people the certainty that they have the skills to operate in the new way. This will include training on:

- What business value looks like. This will be particularly important for first-time employees who won't know what to look for, and the right questions to ask.

- How to use the *why does that matter* question to surface business value from a poor communications brief.

- The difference between business outcomes and outputs.

- The concept that a strategy is a journey with a clear start point and destination.

- The importance of priorities, and how to use them to control what they do.

- The concept of the need to find ways to reach an output or outcome in the smartest way that takes the least time and effort.

  - This should encourage people to recognise that they need to have more knowledge and better skills – to become an EXPERT not just a practitioner.

- How to use new prioritisation tools.

- The difference between economic buyers and user buyers, and how to interact with user buyers.

- How to qualify a brief (both internal and external), so that it's clear/certain what needs to happen next. A clear brief removes the potential for anxiety that the wrong thing will be delivered.
  In the absence of explicit explanations, people often create their own version of the truth. They will then make choices based on what they believe to be the truth of the matter.

(3) **A** is for **AUTONOMY** – a need we have to understand the parameters within which we are expected to operate. This is because our brain wants to know what we can decide for ourselves, and when we need to seek guidance and approval from others.

  If you provide the right training, and clear briefs, to your people, they will welcome the autonomy that comes with finding the smartest way to achieve a client output or outcome. For the online betting client, this would mean giving the team the AUTONOMY to find outlets used by HEBs, and secure coverage that inspires HEBs to click the link and make their first bet.

By providing the clarity that comes with a clear brief – CERTAINTY – you will satisfy their need to feel in control and, therefore, feel able to take decisions. By embedding prioritisation into your approach for clients, you will strengthen this sense of AUTONOMY, because it will be clear that work that doesn't deliver against a priority is not worth doing.

Does this mean that you need to create very tight systems and processes for everything that happens in your business? On the contrary, it means providing very clear parameters within which you give people the freedom to make their own decisions. Providing a strategy expressed as a journey to a destination, with clear steps on the journey, is one example of providing the parameters people need.

By providing your people with CERTAINTY AND AUTONOMY you will give them what they need to be more proactive – an essential requirement for delivering more value from less effort.

FOCUS ON ACHIEVING IMPORTANT CLIENT OUTPUTS AND OUTCOMES NOT USING TIME ON TASKS

One of the most embedded practices within agencies is to allocate each member of the team a certain amount of time to be expended on a client in a given time period. This allocation is often focused on a task, like writing a release or selling in a story.

This practice gets people to focus on the wrong things. It encourages them to use the time they are allocated to carry out the task, rather than achieve important outputs or outcomes. In the case of selling in a story, often this effort will achieve coverage in worthless publications just because it ticks a coverage count target.

If there is a story to sell in, the brief to the individual should be to find a way to secure coverage in a certain number of prioritised target publications. This is not because coverage is the objective but an essential step in the strategy for reaching the destination for the client. It's a step on the journey, with the aim of triggering a specific reaction from the target audience – like clicking a link and making a bet.

The critically important part of the brief is to ask the individual to find the smartest way to achieve the target outputs or outcome, and then stop.

You might allocate a maximum amount of time that is available to achieve the required result. But the expectation will be that the outcome will be achieved in much less time than that. This gets the team to recognise three important things:

- They need to have a lot of knowledge – knowledge about the client, the story, and what it represents, and the media. Without this knowledge they will not be able to find the smartest way to deliver the required value.

- That they need to follow Abraham Lincoln's example and *sharpen their axe* before starting.

- That their time is a precious asset which needs to be used intelligently to deliver value for clients and the agency.

USE A CLIENT'S BUSINESS PRIORITIES TO CONTROL WHAT IS DONE AND WHAT IS NOT DONE

Throughout the book I have stressed the importance of prioritisation. Helping clients to identify priorities was one of the reasons why the Growth Share Matrix was such a success for BCG.

To make the transformation from selling time to value, it will be essential to put prioritisation at the heart of your HOW – the way you deliver value to clients.

Having clear priorities is very empowering. It gives your team the CERTAINTY AND AUTONOMY they need to perform at their best. Failing to satisfy the needs of SCARF will trigger a *'threat'* response in the brain. This impairs cognitive performance, reduces the ability to make decisions, communicate and solve problems – in short, it makes it very hard for people to perform at their best and achieve the results required.

By using the SCARF framework effectively, you will be more certain of triggering a *'reward'* response in the brain. This will automatically make your people willing to do difficult things, to take risks, to think deeply about issues and develop new solutions. And, the reward response is also closely linked to positive emotions, such as: interest, happiness, joy and desire.

Put another way, surfacing clear client priorities, and making sure these are used to control the work that is done, satisfies many of the needs of SCARF and creates happier and more productive people.

To make it easier to focus on priorities, it makes sense to give your people simple prioritisation tools like those in Chapter Five.

HELPING THE TEAM TO CONTROL THE USER BUYER'S NEED FOR 'MORE'

Because user buyers focus on activity rather than value, they have a habit of asking for 'more' in the belief that 'more' of anything delivers value.

This is one of the drivers of the scope creep that dilutes the perception of value delivered by the agency and leads to overservicing and low team morale. We run regular client feedback surveys for clients, and a user buyer's desire for 'more' can be seen in the answer to the question: *'What one thing can we do to increase the value we deliver to your business?'*

Here are three answers from a recent survey.

- *'Get coverage in more titles'.*

- *'More storytelling content'.*

- *'Post more often on our social channels'.*

Economic buyers have very different answers, such as:

- *'Help us generate revenue in a tougher market'.*

- *'Help us achieve our sales targets'.*

- *'Help us attract the talent we need to grow'.*

For the team to be able to sell value, they will need to be able to 'train' user buyers to focus on value too. This requires them to do two important things on a continuous basis:

(1) Use the prioritisation approach and tools to discourage user buyers from asking for things to be done that will not aid the achievement of agreed outputs or outcomes.

   - This will require your people to be skilled at 'saying no'. The priorities and tools will help, but they need to be backed up by a well-practiced communications approach to saying no, in a way that enhances rather than undermines the relationship.

- This will require specific training on how to say no. It will also require very explicit guidance on how your team is allowed to 'push back'. The clarity that this provides will satisfy the need for CERTAINTY AND AUTONOMY and empower your people to be more in control of the day-to-day relationship with their user buyers.

(2) Selling back the value of what has been delivered, and where you are on the journey to the client's destination, at every opportunity.

- One of the best ways to create supportive user buyers is to show them that you want to do two important things:

  - Make their job easier.

  - Make them look good to the senior people in their own organisation.

- To achieve the second goal – making user buyers look good (and through that making your agency look good too) – it is important to explain that you will provide them with regular proof of the value you are achieving together, so they can share that with senior colleagues in their organisation.

- There are two main ways your team should do this:

  - By creating an economic buyer report that highlights the value delivered to the organisation, and sending this on a regular basis – at least quarterly.

  - By highlighting how a particular action, or output, is significant in moving the client closer to the destination. This is best done when it happens, as it shows that there is real progress being made between the regular reporting cycle. I recommend this is done verbally and via email. The most important thing to convey will be the progress towards the destination – not just the result. This gives the user buyer confidence in the work, and the content they need to build confidence internally, if they are asked about progress. It also has a positive impact on your team by acknowledging value has been delivered – thus energising them to keep focused on reaching the client's destination.

MAKE SURE YOU PROVIDE 1-2-1 COACHING ON A REGULAR BASIS

If you have freed time by changing the way you run meetings and other processes, you will be able to coach the team on a frequent basis to hasten the change in their behaviour.

To drive behaviour change, frequency of contact and coaching is essential. This is because people don't know what they don't know and will benefit from being given answers when they confront something for the first time. If they aren't given the support they need during this transformation, they are very likely to revert to what they see as the comfort of the time-based approach.

A very good focus for this coaching will be to help the team persuade the user buyer that regular reports could be streamlined, so that the insights they provide are easier to consume, and so that the team can put maximum effort into value-producing activity.

If you want your team to embrace a value-based approach, you first need to get them in a value-focused frame of mind, and then coach them to deliver the new approach with confidence and belief.

CHECKLIST

(1) Have you explained to your people why you are making the change to selling value not time – and the benefits to them of doing so?

(2) Have you used the SCARF framework to make sure you satisfy the needs our brains have to feel a valued and valuable contributor to this transformation?

(3) Have you explained what this will mean to every individual in terms of their work and job role?

(4) Have you provided all the training needed for people to feel in control of what they are doing?

(5) Have you explained the difference between supplying a user buyer report and selling back value?

(6) Have you shown the team how to sell back the value delivered on a regular basis?

(7) Are you providing the team with frequent 1-2-1 coaching to build their confidence, and help make the change in their behaviour permanent?

11

HOW TO MOVE EXISTING CLIENTS FROM TIME TO VALUE

If you have decided to transform the performance of your business by adopting a *progressive* approach that eliminates wasted time, and offers clients greater certainty of outcomes, you will need to bring your current clients with you on your journey.

This chapter provides some steps to follow.

THE ATTITUDES OF USER AND ECONOMIC BUYERS

Let's look at the attitudes to time of both the economic and user buyer, and what this means to moving from time to value.

(1) User buyers care about how the agency will help them do their job. They look at things from an activity perspective – WHAT is done not WHY it is done. They don't care how long an agency spends on the activities – just that they are done. But because agencies present them with a bank of time, and say that the bank is replenished every month, user buyers think that there is always time available to them. It's like having a magic pot that gets topped up every month.

Consequently, they see a retainer as something that provides the same level of work each month, just because agencies invoice monthly.

By moving to a value-based approach, you instantly remove this constantly replenished bank of time. So, you need to replace it with an approach that reassures them that you will be even more helpful to them AND that you will make them look good to their boss and other senior people in the organisation.

You will need to train them to expect peaks and troughs of activity according to what it takes to deliver agreed priority outcomes.

(2) Economic buyers care about achieving business goals. They create a budget to pay for services that will help them achieve a specific business outcome. They expect a return on investment (ROI).

As far as they are concerned, time is irrelevant. And therefore, time-based reporting is irrelevant. They are paying money for an outcome to be delivered – or for a contribution to be made that will make the outcome more certain.

This latter point is very important for agencies. Economic buyers will understand that an agency will rarely be the only contributor to achieving an outcome, so what they will need to see is how, when and where the agency will contribute to making an outcome more certain.

If presented with an activity list as proof of value, not only will they reject it, but it will reinforce their view that the money spent with the agency may not deliver an effective ROI. That doesn't mean that an economic buyer won't acknowledge a great piece of press coverage. They quite often do, but usually only if someone has made the connection between the coverage and something they value, like a prospect being in contact.

The reality is that the buyer who matters most, when it comes to winning and retaining a client, is the economic buyer. They will very readily embrace a value-based approach because it satisfies their need to see a ROI.

Because they are looking for certainty of a ROI, it makes sense to keep them up to date on your progress towards achieving the desired outcome.

WHAT CAN BE DONE TO MOVE CURRENT CLIENTS FROM TIME TO VALUE?

For current clients there are a range of options for making this transformation. These include:

(1) Using contract renewal as the trigger for moving to a value-based approach. To do this you will need to do the following:

- Use the renewal as a reason to seek clarity on the current business objectives. You could do this as part of a special prioritisation work-shop with the economic buyer, to emphasise your focus on delivering value to the business. Make sure you capture the data you need to understand the value of reaching the desired outcome.

- Show the client a 'picture' of their current position and 'paint' a picture of the destination based on what is shared in the prioritisation workshop.

- Present a strategy for filling the gap from the start point to the destination and emphasise where you will deliver a valuable contribution. This will include highlighting the barriers you will overcome on the way, and how significant those barriers are.

- Quantify the value of your contribution – see Chapter Nine.

- Introduce economic buyer reports a few months ahead of renewal, so that you build a strong perception of your value to the business ahead of renewal. To do this you may need to make some assumptions about what is valued most. Using the online betting example, you could approach the user buyer on the premise of your desire to create an interim report that makes them look good and ask for some data such as: the number of HEBs delivered by links so far, and the average spend of HEBs.

(2) Using a separate project to introduce value pricing – then using the success of the project to encourage a complete change. To do this you will need to do the following:

- Seek clarity on the business objectives for the project. You can get the user buyer to support this approach by showing how it will make them look good. This is important because user buyers are often resistant to extra projects because they see them as extra work that might not make their life easier.

- Show the client a 'picture' of their current position and 'paint' a picture of the destination for the project.

- Present a strategy for filling the gap from the start point to the destination and emphasise where you will deliver a valuable contribution.

- Quantify the value of your contribution.

- Provide both an economic buyer report and a user buyer report.

- Provide a proactive proposal for following the same approach for the work covered by the retainer.

(3) Starting to use the prioritisation tools in Chapter Five to educate the client about a smarter way of making the user buyer's life easier, and increasing the certainty of delivering what the economic buyer needs.

- This can be presented as something you are introducing to all clients because you have been encouraged to do so by other clients.

- You could make this suggestion after running a client feedback survey and attribute the shift to client feedback.

(4) Selling back the business value delivered by adding a companion report to the usual time-based report – as suggested in point 1 above. This would be an economic buyer-friendly summary, most likely delivered as a two-minute video. This progressive transformation provides the time to educate the client about the benefits of the new approach, so that they welcome the shift when it comes.

WHAT DO YOU NEED TO DO TO PREPARE YOUR PEOPLE, SO THEY CAN MAKE THE TRANSFORMATION WORK?

If you want the approaches above to work, you will first need to train all your people:

(1) On the difference between user buyers and economic buyers.

(2) On what a business outcome looks like.

(3) To use the *why does this matter question* to identify the economic driver for a client, even if it hasn't been shared in the communications brief.

(4) To use the prioritisation tools you have created.

(5) To capture and record economic buyer-friendly data.

(6) To create high-impact economic buyer reports.

If you want to shift current clients from time to value, you will need to create the tools to do so and train your people on WHY they are essential and HOW to use them effectively.

CHECKLIST

(1) Have you trained all your people on the difference between user buyers and economic buyers?

(2) Have you trained your people on what a business outcome looks like, and how by using the *why does this matter* question, they can identify what may be the economic driver for a client even if it hasn't been shared in the communications brief?

(3) Have you created simple visual prioritisation tools?

(4) Have you trained your team on how to use the prioritisation tools?

(5) Have you created economic buyer reports in a high impact, visual and shareable format?

(6) Have you been very EXPLICIT with your user buyer about your desire to make them look good, so that you get their buy-in to sharing economic buyer reports throughout their organisation?

(7) Have you created an approach for a prioritisation workshop and practiced how to deliver it?

I hope you have found this book useful in making your transformation from selling time to selling value. If you would like to discuss anything that is covered in the book, please contact me at crispin.manners@onva.co.uk

12

THE CHECKLISTS NEEDED TO MAKE THE TRANSFORMATION TO SELLING VALUE A SUCCESS

This chapter provides all the chapter summaries in one place, so you can use them to implement the transformation within your agency. I hope you will give the book to your teams to use and reuse as they go on the transformation journey.

Remember that making the switch will make your business significantly more profitable from much less effort.

DON'T UNDERSELL THE VALUE YOU CONTRIBUTE TO CLIENTS

On one of my courses, the Managing Director of an agency that focuses on the built environment, said that she quite often helped clients get development approval without the need to go to committee stage. But by doing so, she felt she was losing out on fees needed to support the client through the committee process. What she was saying was that she would charge a fee for the work up to early approval, and if early approval wasn't granted, charge an additional fee.

This is a classic example of an agency being constrained by the time-based model.

If we look at this from a value-based pricing perspective, the outcome the client is paying for is approval, so the price should be the same for early approval or for approval after committee scrutiny. To be clear, I mean the full fee covers the process including the committee stage and is paid if early approval is secured. The agency could then use their expert status and record of securing early approval as another reason for a premium price. If early approval is secured, both the client and the agency are saved from going through the pain of the committee process. And this gives the agency an extra incentive to secure early approval because they secure the full fee without the effort required by the committee activity. But if the committee stage work is required, the agency is not worse off as the full fee took account of the extra effort required.

ONCE YOU OPEN YOUR EYES TO SELLING VALUE, YOU WILL SEE HOW OTHER ORGANISATIONS ARE DOING IT FOR MAXIMUM ADVANTAGE

Another agency owner gave me an example of how one organisation, not a PR agency, charged one of their clients £300,000 for something she had charged another client £60,000. Her approach had been time based, and she realised that she had left £240,000 on the table because the other company had proven what clients were really prepared to pay for the value delivered!

Before you construct a value-based price, make sure you look at what other organisations are charging for delivering similar value in the same sector. It may mean you don't walk past a significant profit opportunity.

If you embrace selling value, there is no reason why – like Boston Consulting Group – you cannot be recognised as a world-class agency that is sought out by the clients you most aspire to work with.

CHECKLIST – THE EIGHT DEADLY SINS OF TIME-BASED PRICING

(1) Have you identified the outcome the client values most, that they are hiring you to help deliver?

(2) Have you developed a clear strategy for how you will deliver that outcome, and have you linked the price to the outcome and the strategy?

(3) Have you explicitly identified your part in delivering the desired outcome?

(4) Have you captured how you will deliver that outcome in an explicit SOW?

(5) Have you captured what is not included in a companion document to the SOW?

(6) Have you identified the value that the client expects to be delivered in terms of the outcomes they expect, and the outputs which are important steps on the journey to the outcome?

(7) Have you identified the client's top three business priorities?

(8) Have you allocated team tasks based on achieving the agreed outcomes, outputs and priorities – with the expectation that this is achieved in the least amount of time?

(9) Have you identified your major time drains, and calculated the cost to the business of not addressing them?

(10) Have you created effective replacement processes to the time drains you eliminate?

(11) Have you given a clear brief on the outcomes and outputs to be delivered?

CHECKLIST – THE IMPORTANCE OF IDENTIFYING THE VALUE CLIENTS WANT

(1) Have you identified the business outcome the client is hiring you to help deliver?

(2) Have you quantified the business/financial value to the client of achieving that outcome?

(3) Have you identified the important steps to be taken to achieve that outcome?

(4) Have you identified what value you contribute at each of those steps?

(5) Have you established the importance of your contribution to each of those steps, as compared to other potential contributors? If you show a better return, the client will choose you.

(6) Have you captured proof of the value you have delivered for this client, and other clients, so you can create a sense of certainty that the value will be delivered if the client chooses you?

(7) Do you practice self-acknowledgement about the value you deliver, so you build confidence and belief in your ability to command a premium price?

(8) Do you have an explicit way of doing things that makes the delivery of the value the client expects more certain?

CHECKLIST – THE IMPORTANCE OF BEING 'MARMITE NOT VANILLA'

(1) Have you calculated the cost of a complex pitch?

(2) Have you calculated the cost of losing, and used this as a motivator to surface the value you deliver to clients?

(3) Have you identified what you believe in as the foundation for the value you want your agency to deliver?

(4) Have you identified the clients, and the work, that energises you most – and why that is the case?

(5) Have you captured your WHY in an 'I believe' statement that would resonate with your people and your clients?

(6) Have you tested your WHY by asking: 'why does that matter' until you reach the highest level of value possible.

CHECKLIST – WHY IT'S IMPORTANT TO EXPLAIN HOW VALUE IS DELIVERED IN A WAY THAT IS UNIQUE TO YOUR AGENCY

(1) Does your approach focus on delivering business OUTCOMES and not just communications OUTPUTS?

(2) Have you brought the approach you use to the surface, and packaged it as a methodology?

(3) Have you checked that you aren't describing your approach in the language other agencies use?

(4) Have you given your method a name – so that you can accentuate your expert status by promoting the power of your branded method?

(5) Does your HOW link to your WHY, and build confidence and belief in your ability to deliver your WHY?

(6) Have you brought your method to life by embedding it in existing case studies?

(7) Have you identified the clients, and the work, that energises you most – and why that is the case?

(8) Does your HOW increase CERTAINTY for the client?

(9) Does your HOW help the client to PRIORITISE action?

(10) Have you captured your HOW in simple, visual tools?

CHECKLIST – HOW TO CREATE THE TOOLS THAT BRING YOUR BRANDED METHOD TO LIFE AND GIVE YOUR TEAM WAYS TO REINFORCE IT

(1) Have you identified the key steps in your methodology and how each step can be supported by specific visual tools?

(2) Have you checked that the tools you create help you to avoid describing your approach in the language other agencies use?

(3) Have you identified tools that enable you to involve your clients at key stages in the development of your strategy so that they become committed to your strategy?

(4) Do your tools satisfy the clients' need for prioritisation, and make everything you do focus on delivering client outcomes in the most effective way – thus reducing or eliminating overservicing?

CHECKLIST – HOW TO CREATE PREMIUM PRICED SERVICES THAT BREAK THE TIME TO PRICE EQUATION

(1) Do you bring the valuable outputs and outcomes you achieve to the surface?

(2) Do you quantify the value of the outputs and outcomes in a way that is meaningful to the client?

(3) Do you accentuate the expert knowledge and skills of all your people in a way that reinforces your HOW?

(4) Do you enable you and your people to behave like experts?

(5) Have you developed the tools that reinforce their expertise?

(6) Have you separated your 'sharpening the axe' services from the amorphous mire of a retainer?

(7) Do you use your premium priced, expert services to build confidence and belief in all your services?

(8) Do you use your premium priced expert services to open doors with the clients you most want to work with?

(9) Do you use your premium priced expert services to build a healthy revenue and profit stream that breaks the time to price equation?

CHECKLIST – HOW TO SET A VALUE-BASED PRICE

(1) Have you asked the questions that enable you to calculate the value of a client's business objective?

(2) Have you identified the strategic importance of achieving that objective?

(3) Have you identified the alternative approaches being used, and the cost of alternative approaches?

(4) Have you identified the performance of existing approaches, and captured the data associated with this performance?

(5) Have you identified the steps on the journey to the objective/outcome where you can provide the most value?

(6) Have you made explicit to the client your contribution, and HOW you will deliver it?

(7) Have you built a strong perception of your expert knowledge, skills and methodology to be able to command a premium?

(8) Have you quantified the value of achieving parts of the objective, to create the foundation for your price?

(9) Have you made it easy to accept your price, by showing how your contribution delivers more value than the alternative options?

CHECKLIST – THE IMPORTANCE OF ACCESS TO CLIENT DATA THAT
IDENTIFIES AND PROVES THE VALUE YOU DELIVER

(1) Have you surfaced the WHY behind the WHAT – i.e. converted a WHAT brief into a WHY brief?

(2) Have you quantified the financial value of reaching the destination – achieving the WHY?

(3) Have you quantified the strategic value of reaching the destination – achieving the WHY?

(4) Have you identified the steps on the journey where you contribute?

(5) Have you quantified the starting point, and therefore the gap, and the financial value of filling the gap to the destination?

(6) Have you identified how the client measures success, and the data they use to do that?

(7) Have you explained the benefit to the individual (the user buyer) and the organisation (the economic buyer) of sharing this data with you?

(8) Have you used the data that is captured to crystallise and sell back the value that you deliver?

CHECKLIST – HOW YOUR TEAM CAN GET THE USER BUYER TO
EMBRACE A VALUE-BASED APPROACH

(1) Have you established the client's business objectives at the outset, and prioritised them with the client?

(2) Have you connected clear communications objectives to each business objective, and prioritised them?

(3) Have you changed what is 'counted' by user buyers, so they understand their requests for more activity results in less rather than more value?

(4) Have you captured the priorities in visual tools like those shown in Chapter Eight?

(5) Have you captured the starting position for the client in an infographic that can be used thereafter to show the difference the agency has made?

(6) Have you captured the destination for the client in an infographic that quantifies the value that reaching the destination will deliver?

(7) Have you agreed which data needs to be provided to quantify what is being delivered for each of the priorities?

(8) Are you using the priorities, the picture of the destination and data to stop scope creep and keep the user buyer focused on business priorities?

(9) Are you providing an economic buyer-friendly report to share with senior stakeholders in the organisation that shows the value delivered to the organisation in a high impact, visual and sharable format?

(10) Have you explained to the user buyer that the economic buyer report is your investment to make them look good (and the agency), by making EXPLICIT their contribution to achieving the organisation's business objectives?

(11) Are you revisiting the priorities on a quarterly basis to ensure that all work is focused on delivering the most valued and valuable outcomes?

CHECKLIST – HOW TO CHANGE THE DAY-TO-DAY BEHAVIOUR OF ACCOUNT TEAMS TO SUPPORT THE VALUE-BASED PRICING APPROACH

(1) Have you explained to your people why you are making the change to selling value not time – and the benefits to them of doing so?

(2) Have you used the SCARF framework to make sure you satisfy the needs our brains have to feel a valued and valuable contributor to this transformation?

(3) Have you explained what this will mean to every individual in terms of their work and job role?

(4) Have you provided all the training needed for people to feel in control of what they are doing?

(5) Have you explained the difference between supplying a user buyer report and selling back value?

(6) Have you shown the team how to sell back the value delivered on a regular basis?

(7) Are you providing the team with frequent 1-2-1 coaching to build their confidence, and help make the change in their behaviour permanent?

CHECKLIST – HOW TO MOVE EXISTING CLIENTS FROM TIME TO VALUE

(1) Have you trained all your people on the difference between user buyers and economic buyers?

(2) Have you trained your people on what a business outcome looks like, and how by using the *why does this matter* question, they can identify what may be the economic driver for a client even if it hasn't been shared in the communications brief?

(3) Have you created simple visual prioritisation tools?

(4) Have you trained your team on how to use the prioritisation tools?

(5) Have you created economic buyer reports in a high impact, visual and shareable format?

(6) Have you been very EXPLICIT with your user buyer about your desire to make them look good, so that you get their buy-in to sharing economic buyer reports throughout their organisation?

(7) Have you created an approach for a prioritisation workshop and practiced how to deliver it?

REFERENCE LIST

INTRODUCTION

(1) The Public Relations and Communications Association in the UK. https://newsroom.prca.org.uk/pressreleases/more-than-a-half-of-pr-agencies-to-increase-fees-prca-icco-confidence-tracker-3215837
(2) The Worldcom Confidence Index is a 'living' tracker of what 80,000 global CEOs are writing about. https://worldcomgroup.com/confidence-index/2022-reports/
(3) Roaring out of recession by Ranjay Gulati, Nitin Nohria, and Franz Wohlgezogen. The Harvard Business Review March 2010. https://hbr.org/2010/03/roaring-out-of-recession

CHAPTER 1

(1) PR's overservicing epidemic: 90% of agencies overservice client accounts. https://www.prweek.com/article/1667069/prs-overservicing-epidemic-90-agencies-overservice-client-accounts
(2) PRCA Agency Barometer Report 2022. https://www.mynewsdesk.com/uk/prca/pressreleases/prca-agency-barometer-report-client-budgets-increasing-as-pr-emerges-from-pandemic-3188618

CHAPTER 2

(1) Ibis World – Public Relations & Communication Activities in the UK – Market Size 2011–2029. https://www.ibisworld.com/united-kingdom/market-size/public-relations-communication-activities/

(2) Ibis World – Public Relations Firms in the US – Market Size 2002–2028. https://www.ibisworld.com/industry-statistics/market-siz e/public-relations-firms-united-states/

CHAPTER 3

(1) Marmite is a food brand marketed by Unilever PLC. https://www.u-nilever.co.uk/brands/nutrition/marmite/
(2) See the Cambridge Dictionary definition of Marmite. https://dictio-nary.cambridge.org/dictionary/english/marmite
(3) Greenhouse. https://www.greenhouse.agency/what-we-do-impactful-communications-campaigns/
(4) 90ten. https://90ten.co.uk/
(5) Playtime PR. https://www.playtimepr.com/
(6) Alice PR and Events. https://alicepr.com/
(7) PRCA training. https://www.prca.org.uk/event/5056/managing-an-agency-%E2%80%93-part-1

CHAPTER 4

(1) Cause UK. https://www.causeuk.com/
(2) No Brainer Agency. https://www.nobraineragency.co.uk/
(3) Alice PR and Events. https://alicepr.com/
(4) What Is the Growth Share Matrix? https://www.bcg.com/about/overview/our-history/growth-share-matrix
(5) The image of the Growth Share Matrix is provided courtesy of Boston Consulting Group (BCG)
(6) Inspiring Workplaces Group. https://www.inspiring-workplaces.com/

CHAPTER 5

(1) Dr Robert B Cialdini author of Influence: The Psychology of Persuasion. Publisher: HarperCollins Publishers Inc.

CHAPTER 6

(1) Dr Robert B Cialdini author of Influence: The Psychology of Persuasion. Publisher: HarperCollins Publishers Inc.

CHAPTER 10

(1) Dr David Rock: David Rock SCARF: A brain-based model for collaborating with and influencing others. https://davidrock.net/

INDEX